Making the Most of Your Android Phone

Jim Gatenby

BERNARD BABANI (publishing) LTD
The Grampians
Shepherds Bush Road
London W6 7NF
England

www.babanibooks.com

D0599910

Please Note

Although every care has been taken with the production of this book to ensure that all information is correct at the time of writing and that any projects, designs, modifications and/ or programs, etc., contained herewith, operate in a correct and safe manner and also that any components specified are normally available in Great Britain, the Publishers and Author do not accept responsibility in any way for the failure (including fault in design) of any project, design, modification or program to work correctly or to cause damage to any equipment that it may be connected to or used in conjunction with, or in respect of any other damage or injury that may be so caused, nor do the Publishers accept responsibility in any way for the failure to obtain specified components.

Notice is also given that if equipment that is still under warranty is modified in any way or used or connected with home-built equipment then that warranty may be void.

© 2018 BERNARD BABANI (publishing) LTD

First Published – May 2018

British Library Cataloguing in Publication Data:
A catalogue record for this book is available from the British Library

ISBN 978-0-85934-773-0
Cover Design by Gregor Arthur
Printed and bound in Great Britain for Bernard Babani (publishing) Ltd

About this Book

In 2017 the Android operating system was used in over 85% of the world's smartphones. Some manufacturers modify the Android user interface to suit their own needs but even these "tweaked" versions still have much in common with the standard Android.

This book has been prepared using the very popular Motorola Moto G 5 and Samsung Galaxy smartphones. The Moto G 5 is a budget phone running the standard or "stock" version of the Android operating system. The Samsung Galaxy is a "top of the range" phone with a more colourful user interface. This is illustrated in the two extracts from their respective **Settings** screens shown below.

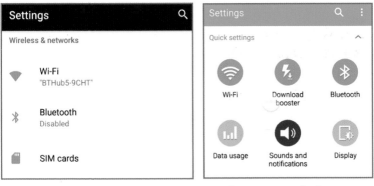

Stock Android   Samsung Galaxy

Although the two versions of the Android operating system in the above examples are quite different in appearance, the contents and functions are the same.

Similarly, although the stock Android itself has evolved through many editions, such as the three latest, Marshmallow, Nougat and Oreo, the material in this book should apply to Android phones in general.

One of the aims of this book is to show that the Android smartphone is as powerful as its larger relative, the tablet, as well as other computers such as laptops.

Android 5 inch smartphone

Android 9 inch tablet

The smartphone is also more versatile than the standard tablet, as discussed below:

- The smartphone can make phone calls and send text messages. Most standard tablets can't be used as a phone in this way.

- The smartphone can connect to the Internet in places where there is no Wi-Fi, using a *cell phone network*. The standard tablet is *Wi-Fi only*.

- The smartphone has all the computing capability of the tablet (and larger computers) to browse the Web, send e-mails, play music and videos, store photos in the "clouds" and use social networks, etc., etc.

- Powerful apps or software such as Microsoft Word and Excel and eBooks are now available for smartphones. Despite the small screen size these are quite useable on the smartphone.

- The smartphone is smaller, lighter and more portable.

There are two main sections to this book:

- Chapters 1-7 describe setting up a new Android smartphone and using it as a mobile phone.
- Chapters 8-14 describe the use of the smartphone like a tablet for a wide range of computing tasks,

The book starts off with an overview of the Android phone, its uses, technical specification and its main components. The use of SIM cards and the way they are used to connect the phone to 3G/4G cellular networks such as Three, EE, O2 and Vodafone are then described. The options for subscribing to a network are discussed such as monthly contracts and Pay As You Go plans giving allowances for phone calls, text messages and Internet *data plans*.

The Android Setup Wizard is described, including connecting to your Wi-Fi network and creating a *Google account*, essential for many important activities. Making and receiving phone calls and sending text messages are discussed in detail.

Chapter 8 describes the use of the smartphone in its role as a computer, with touch screen gestures, on-screen keyboard and *voice recognition*. Navigating the various screens as well as managing apps installed from the Play Store are also covered.

Later chapters cover computing activities such as browsing the Web, e-mail, social networking, eBooks, music, videos and live and catchup television.

The final chapter covers *cloud computing* for the backing up and sharing of files, accessible to any computer, anywhere. Also *printing* to a remote printer and using *mobile data* and *mobile hotspots* to connect to the Internet over a mobile phone network. Finally, the dangers of *data roaming*, followed by security and tracing a lost or stolen phone are described.

About the Author

Jim Gatenby trained as a Chartered Mechanical Engineer and initially worked at Rolls-Royce Ltd using computers in the analysis of jet engine performance. He obtained a Master of Philosophy degree in Mathematical Education by research at Loughborough University of Technology and taught mathematics and computing in school for many years before becoming a full-time author. The author has written over fifty books in the fields of educational computing, Android tablets and smartphones and Microsoft Windows, including many of the titles in the highly successful "Older Generation" series from Bernard Babani (publishing) Ltd, all of which have been very well received.

Trademarks

Android, Google, Google Drive, Chrome, Gmail, Google Cloud Print and YouTube are trademarks or registered trademarks of Google, Inc. Facebook is a registered trade mark of Facebook, Inc. Twitter is a registered trademark of Twitter, Inc. WhatsApp is a trademark or registered trademark of WhatsApp, Inc. Instagram is a trademark or registered trademark of Instagram, Inc. Snapchat is a trademark or registered trademark of Snap, Inc. HP Print Service Plugin and HP ePrint are trademarks or registered trademarks of HP, Inc. All other brand and product names used in this book are recognized as trademarks or registered trademarks, of their respective companies.

Acknowledgements

I would like to thank my wife Jill for her support during the preparation of this book and also Michael Babani for making the project possible.

Contents

6

7

11

12

Much More Than a Phone

Introduction

In recent years sales of Android smartphones have outstripped the sales of tablets, laptops and desktop computers. Advantages of Android smartphones compared with these other computers include the following:

- The smartphone is a multi–purpose device. As well as being your main phone, it can serve as a capable and versatile computer.

- Smartphones are relatively inexpensive.

- They are small, light and very easily portable in a pocket or handbag.

- Where there is no Wi-Fi you can connect to the Internet using your cell phone network, (Unlike most tablets and laptops, which can only use Wi-Fi).

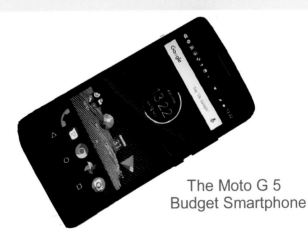

The Moto G 5
Budget Smartphone

The Android Operating System

Android is the name of the *operating system*, i.e. the software or programs used to control the main functions of a computer, such as the touch screen user interface and the screen display. Android is owned by Google, Inc. and new versions are regularly launched. Each version of Android operates similarly and is named after confectionery; recent versions include Android 6 Marshmallow and Android 7 Nougat. At the time of writing, the latest version, Android 8 Oreo, is not yet widely available. The Android logo is shown on the right.

Android Smartphone Brands

Android smartphones are marketed by a number of well established companies such as Google, Samsung, Sony, LG, HTC and Motorola. While individual companies may add some features of their own, the underlying operating system is basically the same on all brands of Android.

Smartphones vs Tablets

The smartphone is a mobile phone which also has all the main functions of a tablet, such as browsing the Internet, social networking, e-mail, television, radio and two cameras for taking photos and making videos.

Smartphones typically have a diagonal screen size of around 4 inches up to a maximum of 7 inches. Large smartphones with screen sizes above 5.5 inches are known as *phablets*.

Most Android tablets have a screen size of 7, 8, 9 or 10 inches. Large tablets with a separate keyboard are also known as *hybrid* or *2-in-1* computers. Obviously the larger screen size of the tablet and optional keyboard make it more suitable for working with large documents, etc.

The SIM Card

Unlike most tablets, many smartphones have a *SIM Card* or *Subscriber Identity Module,* a small plastic card containing a microchip storing your phone number, contacts list, text messages and other information about your phone service. You may be able to remove the SIM card and use it in another phone, as discussed shortly.

3G and 4G Networks

3G and *4G* are the latest generations of *cell phone networks*, consisting of cells of towers around the country, used by EE, O2, Giffgaff, BT Mobile, Sky Mobile, etc.

- The Android smartphone phone connects to the 3G or 4G network to make phone calls.

- The smartphone can also use the 3G or 4G network to connect to the Internet wherever there is a phone signal. Then it can be used as a computer for Web browsing, e-mail, social networking, etc., etc.

- Some tablet computers have 3G or 4G connectivity but they are relatively expensive and too large to hold to your ear and use as a normal phone.

Wi-Fi

Wi-Fi provides wireless connections to the Internet, often using a *router*, a device provided by an *Internet Service Provider* such as BT or Sky, etc. The router connects to the telephone landline in your home. Wi-Fi connections are also provided in cafes, hotels and on trains and buses, etc.

- Android phones can use both Wi-Fi and 3G/4G. They can automatically switch between 3G/4G and Wi-Fi (where available) to get the best connection.

- Wi-Fi Internet access is cheaper then 3G and 4G.

Using the Smartphone as a Cell Phone

All of the activities on the smartphone such as making a phone call, browsing the Internet, playing music or taking a photograph are launched by tapping an icon for the relevant *app* or *program*. There are several Home and Apps screens containing your apps and these are discussed in detail shortly. A phone call is started by tapping the phone icon shown on the right and below. Although there are slight differences in the appearance of the phone icons on different systems, they are otherwise the same.

Phone

Phone   Messages   Chrome   Photos   Apps

Android 6 Marshmallow on Samsung Galaxy

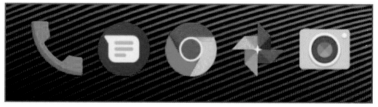

Android 7 Nougat on Moto G5

As shown above, different manufacturers may tweak the colour schemes and screen designs, but the icons for most apps are the same or very similar in all brands. This also applies across different versions of the Android operating system, such as Marshmallow and Nougat shown above.

Tapping the phone icon opens the window shown below, with an icon to open the **Keypad** to enter a phone number to call. The **Log** icon below displays a list of previous calls. **Favorites** also shown below lists the numbers you call frequently and **Contacts** is the complete list of the people you call.

Making and receiving phone calls is discussed in more detail in Chapter 6.

The Smartphone as a Powerful Computer

The Android smartphone is very much more than a device for making phone calls to your friends. It's also a powerful and versatile computer with access to millions of apps and videos for entertainment, work and education, etc., etc.

Google Software

Google, the owner and developer of Android, itself pre-installs a range of *apps* (the modern name for *applications software*) for a variety of tasks, as shown in the samples below. These include the famous Google search engine used by billions of people to "Google" for information on the Internet. This makes the latest information, on every conceivable subject, easily available.

Pre-installed Software

In addition to the Google apps, you need software to perform the particular tasks you wish to do, such as sending an e-mail, playing music or reading an eBook, for example.

When you buy a new smartphone, many popular and useful apps are pre-installed, as shown on the next page. (Some versions of Android, such as Marshmallow, use a white background, but are essentially the same otherwise).

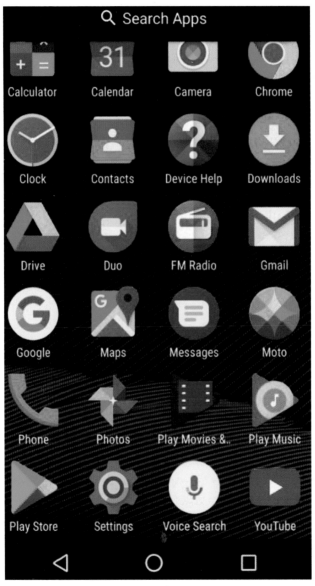

Pre-installed Apps
Android 7 Nougat on Moto G5

Some Popular Apps

Apps appear as icons on several Apps screens, as shown in the example on the previous page. Listed below are some very popular and useful Android apps, together with their icons. Many of these are pre-installed or, if not, can easily be installed from the Play Store, discussed on page 11.

Play Store

The **Play Store** icon gives access to over 3 million apps in different categories. These are either free or can be bought online for a few pounds. When a new app is installed its icon appears on the Home and Apps screens.

Google

Google is a famous *search engine*. "To Google" means to search for information on a particular subject, after typing in some relevant *keywords*. Google also includes *voice search* for entering the keywords by speaking.

Chrome

Google Chrome is a *Web browser*, similar to Microsoft Edge, Internet Explorer and Apple Safari. A Web browser is used to display Web pages and to navigate between pages using *links*. You can also revisit Web pages from your *browsing history* or which you've *bookmarked* for future viewing.

Gmail

Google mail or **Gmail** is a free and very popular e-mail service allowing you to send and receive messages consisting of text, pictures and attached files. Creating a Gmail account and password also gives you access to other Google services.

Photos

Google Photos is a photo gallery which saves and organizes all the photos you take using the built-in camera on your phone. Photos are automatically *backed up* on the Internet and can be edited and *shared* with friends.

Earth

Google Earth allows you to zoom in and view maps of different parts of the globe, using satellite images, aerial photography and images captured by cameras mounted on cars all over the world.

Play Books

Play Books allows you to read books in your Library or download new ones from a choice of millions in the Play Store, some of them free.

YouTube

YouTube is a free Google Website which allows individuals and companies to upload and share videos for other people to view. These may include amusing incidents or popular music videos. If a video spreads quickly and is viewed by millions of people, it is said to "go viral".

Play Music

Play Music allows you to shop for music to download to your smartphone or to play tracks already in your Library.

Play Movies & TV

Play Movies & TV is used to download and watch videos and TV shows bought from the Play Store.

Facebook

Facebook is the leading *social networking* Website. Users of Facebook post their *Profile* or *Timeline* on the Internet, allowing them to become online *friends* with people having similar interests. Friends exchange news, information, photographs and videos, etc.

Twitter

Twitter is a popular social networking Website, on which users post short messages or *tweets* (up to 280 characters long) and also can include photos and videos. Celebrities use Twitter to air their views and may have thousands of followers. You can follow whoever you like, reply to *tweets*, or use Twitter for a campaign.

Skype

Skype allows you to make free worldwide voice and video calls over the Internet, between all types of computer. The Skype app is free and Android smartphones have the necessary microphone, speakers and cameras built in.

WhatsApp

WhatsApp is a messaging service for smartphones, which allows free phone calls across the Internet, rather than the cell phone network. You can send and receive text messages, photos, videos and voice messages.

The Google Play Store

Android smartphones have access to over 3 million specially designed apps in the *Google Play Store*. These can be downloaded from the Internet and installed on your phone.

Many of the apps are free or cost just a few pounds. Apps are available for a vast range of subjects, such as Web browsing, free Skype worldwide video calls, Facebook, Twitter, WhatsApp and Instagram social networking. Also for enjoying YouTube videos, music, live and catch up television, online newspapers and games, etc.

The Google Play Store

Android Smartphone Applications

The screen of the smartphone might be too small for writing your memoirs or designing an electric car, for example. However, there is a huge range of tasks, with suitable apps in the Play Store, in addition to those pre-installed, for which the phone is very capable, such as:

- Viewing news, weather and traffic information.

- Sending and receiving e-mails, making Skype video calls and social networking, using Facebook, etc.

- Taking and viewing photos and making videos.

- Enjoying music, live and catch-up TV and radio.

- Reading eBooks and online newspapers.

- Browsing the Internet to find information on any subject — health, holidays, research, homework, etc.

- Playing games.

- Monitoring bank accounts and utilities statements.

- Buying and selling anything online such as books, holidays, travel tickets. Printing boarding passes.

- Monitoring the location, altitude and speed of an airliner in flight, anywhere in the world.

- Ordering meals while seated in a restaurant, for delivery to your table .

- Reading and translating bar codes.

- Displaying maps and acting as a Sat Nav.

- Acting as a *mobile hotspot* to connect a Wi-Fi only device, such as a tablet or laptop, to the Internet via a 3G or 4G cell phone network. (Known as *tethering*).

The Parts of a Smartphone

Introduction

It may be difficult to believe that the small, handheld smartphone is also a powerful computer. As discussed shortly, the main components which affect the speed and performance of a computer are present in the smartphone. So in some respects the smartphone is as powerful as some much larger tablet, laptop and desktop computers.

This chapter discusses the main components of a smartphone. A basic understanding of these is necessary in order to choose a phone that meets your requirements.

The main rival to the Android smartphone is the iPhone made by a single company, the mighty Apple, Inc.

Whereas Android smartphones are marketed by many companies including Samsung, Sony, Motorola, Google, LG, HTC and Huawei. The Android operating system is a Google product and although superficially tweaked by some manufacturers, it is basically the same on all brands of Android phone.

Buying a Smartphone

The two main methods of equipping yourself with a new smartphone are:

- A contract with 12 or 24 monthly payments to cover the price of the phone and the *calls*, *text* and *data*.
- Buying a *SIM-free* phone and inserting a *SIM card* (discussed shortly) for one of the phone networks.

The above purchasing options are discussed in Chapter 3.

Technical Specifications

Shown below are the specifications of two very popular
Android smartphones. The Samsung Galaxy S8 is a top of
the range Android phone, costing around £600 SIM-free.

The Motorola Moto G5 is a popular budget phone costing
around £170-£220 if bought SIM-free. The cheapest budget
phones cost as little as £50, with the fully featured
Vodafone Smart Prime 7 available for just £75.

	Motorola Moto G5	**Samsung Galaxy S8**
Screen size	5.0ins	5.8ins
Android O.S. Planned upgrade	7.0 Nougat 8.0 Oreo	7.0 Nougat 8.0 Oreo
Processor speed	1.4GHz	2.3GHz
Memory (RAM)	2/3GB	4GB
Internal Storage	6/32GB	64GB
Screen resolution	1080x1920 441ppi	1440x2960 570ppi
Front camera Rear camera	5MP 13MP	8MP 12MP
Micro USB port	Yes	Yes
MicroSD card slot	Up to 256MB	Up to 256MB
SIM card (page 18)	Nano-SIM	Nano-SIM

Terms such as MB and GB shown above, used as units
for the storage of *data* inside a computer or moved
around the Internet, are explained on page 15.

Units of Data Storage

The table on page 14 and the notes on page 17 introduce a number of computer storage terms, as explained below.

A computer works on the binary number system consisting only of 0's and 1's, known as *binary digits* or *bits*.

1 *Byte* is a group of 8 bits and can be used to represent a letter of the alphabet or an instruction, for example.

0 1 0 0 0 0 1 1 ⎯ 1 Byte
The Letter C in the Binary Code

1 Kilobyte(KB)	= 1024 Bytes
1 Megabyte(MB)	= 1024 Kilobytes
1 Gigabyte(GB)	= 1024 Megabyte
1 Terabyte(TB)	= 1024 Gigabytes

Examples of Storage Capacities

A few examples are included below to give an idea of the storage space used by data (text, photos, etc.,) when saved as files in the Internal Storage or on a Micro SD card, or moved around the Internet, as discussed on page 17.

- A page of plain text might use 15KB of storage.
- A photo might typically take up 3 to 6 MB of storage.
- Browsing the Web for about 40 hours might use up about 1GB of your data allowance with a network.

To use a phone to store lots of photos, etc., you may wish to pay extra for a model with more Internal Storage and a slot for a Micro SD card, as discussed on page 17.

As can be seen from the table on page 14, the main differences between the budget Moto G5 and the more expensive Galaxy S8 are the processor speed, the amount of Internal Storage, the memory and the screen resolution. The Moto G range uses a standard version of Android while Samsung add some modifications of their own to Android.

If you're not familiar with some of the terms used in the table on page 14, they are explained below.

Processor

This is a chip, also known as the *CPU* (*Central Processing Unit*) which executes the instructions in the current app or program. The speed of a processor is measured in *GHz* (*Gigahertz*). Typical processor speeds are 1.0GHz-2.5GHz. The speed of the processor is based on the speed of a *clock* which generates *pulses* to carry out instructions. Processors may carry out one or more instructions per pulse.

1GHz = 1 billion pulses per second.

Memory or RAM

This is the *volatile* or *temporary* store into which the instructions for the current program are loaded. The memory is cleared when the device is switched off. A shortage of memory causes a computer to run slowly. Typical Android smartphone memory sizes are 2GB-4GB (Gigabytes).

The table on page 14 shows that the performance of the Android smartphone is comparable with that of many bigger computers, where 3-4GB of RAM and processor speeds of 1.0-2.5 GHz are common.

The processor speed and the amount of RAM are critical in the performance of any computer — smartphone, tablet laptop or desktop computer.

Internal Storage

This is not to be confused with the memory or RAM described on page 16. The Internal Storage in a smartphone is a *non-volatile* location where apps and data files such as photos and music are *semi-permanently* saved until wiped or overwritten. It usually takes the form of *flash memory* chips, with typical capacities of 16GB, 32GB and 64GB. Not surprisingly, smartphones with more Internal Storage are more expensive. (Laptop and desktop computers may have 500GB to 1000GB or 1TB (1 Terabyte) of Internal Storage). The Android smartphone compensates for this by saving data in the *Clouds* such as Google Drive, OneDrive and Dropbox, as discussed later.

Micro SD Card

Some smartphones have a slot for a *Micro SD card*, shown on the right, a smaller version of the *SD* (*Secure Digital*) card used in traditional digital cameras. This is used to supplement the Internal Storage. Typical Micro SD card capacities are 8GB, 16GB, 32GB, 64GB, 128GB and 256GB.

The Micro SD card can be inserted into an adapter the size of a standard SD card. So the same Micro SD card can also be used in devices which take a standard SD card, such as larger computers, digital cameras and printers.

Screen size

This is measured diagonally from the top to the bottom of the screen area.

Screen Resolution

The resolution, measured in *pixels* and *pixels per inch*, affects the sharpness and clarity of the display.

SIM Card

As mentioned earlier, the SIM card provides a connection to your cell phone network such as EE or Three and also to the Internet. A contract with a network will often provide a new smartphone including a SIM card. Or you can buy a SIM card and insert it into a new or existing SIM-free phone. As shown below, there are 3 common sizes of SIM card, *standard*, *micro* and *nano*.

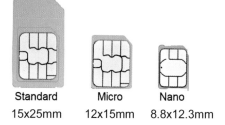

| Standard | Micro | Nano |
| 15x25mm | 12x15mm | 8.8x12.3mm |

These fit into a slot inside the smartphone and SIM cards can easily be swapped between two compatible phones. Different manufacturers may use different slot sizes and obviously a large SIM can't fit into a smaller slot. A small SIM can be used in a larger slot by using a *SIM card adapter* — a frame which surrounds the smaller card.

If buying a new card, the *triple SIM card*, also known as the *Trio* or *3-in-1*, overcomes this problem. This consists of a nano-SIM card within a plastic frame the size of a standard SIM, as shown on the right. The frame can be trimmed to create either a micro-SIM or a nano-SIM.

Dual Sim Cards

Some smartphones have slots for *dual SIM cards*, allowing you to have two phone numbers on one phone, perhaps one for work and one for social calls, for example.

External Features and Controls

The diagram below shows the buttons, connections and other features of an Android smartphone. These are similar on all brands of Android, though the locations of buttons, etc. on individual brands may be different.

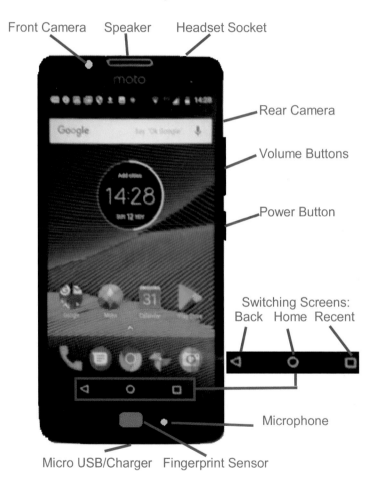

An Android Smartphone

Micro USB Port

This is located as shown on page 19 and used for connecting the battery charger. It's also used to connect the smartphone to a laptop or desktop PC via a *USB cable*, for the transfer of files such as photos, music and documents. The copying of files is done using the *file manager* program on the PC, such as Windows File Explorer.

OTG (On The Go) Cable

The *OTG* cable connects the Micro USB port on the phone to a full size USB device such as an *SD card reader* or a *USB flash drive*. This can be used for the copying of files, such as photos, between the phone and the USB device.

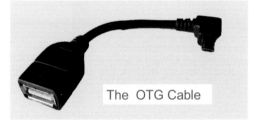

The OTG Cable

File Managers

The Play Store has lots of free file manager apps, such as the examples shown below. These are used to copy files.

USB Media Explor..   ES File Explorer   File Manager

As discussed later in this book, files such as photos and documents, etc., can also be copied easily between your phone and other computers using the Clouds on the Internet such as Google Drive, Dropbox and OneDrive.

Battery

The battery is a critical component in the smartphone. Running out of power when the phone is urgently needed is obviously not acceptable. Many smartphones have a battery life (between charges) of 10-16 hours with a few exceeding 20 hours.

Facebook and other social networks are known to drain the battery quickly, along with high screen brightness and **location** settings. (**Settings** are discussed later in this book).

If you need to use your phone (and all your contacts) in an emergency and you find your battery is flat, it might be possible to remove your SIM card and insert in another compatible phone, as discussed on page 18.

Apart from the mains charger normally supplied with a new phone, inexpensive car battery chargers are available which plug into the car's cigarette lighter socket. So you can keep charging your smartphone while you're travelling.

It's recommended that to extend the overall life (in years) of your battery before it needs replacing, you should try to keep the battery above 50% charged. Also to give it small, regular daily charges rather than a single 100% charge.

Cameras

A front camera, facing the user, allows you to take "selfies" and make video calls with the Skype app, etc. A rear camera allows you to take photos and videos in a similar way to a separate digital camera. The camera resolutions of 12 and 13 *megapixels* (millions of *pixels*, short for *picture elements*) in the table on page 14 show that the rear cameras on these Android smartphones are of a high standard.

The Smartphone vs Larger Computers

In spite of its tiny components, the smartphone can carry out many of the functions performed by some much larger computers, in addition to its role as your main phone. Some key points are:

- Smartphones have processors and RAM (i.e. memory) of a similar technical specification to those in many large computers. These are critical to the performance of any computer.

- Traditional larger computers have used bulky hard disk drives, CD and DVD drives for storing data files and installing new software. The smartphone can back up data to the Clouds and share it with other computers of all types. The Android smartphone can download new software from the Google Play Store.

- The smartphone can display photos and documents, such as a chapter of this book and print them on a wireless printer, just as well as larger computers.

- There are many other computing applications for which the smartphone is more than capable, such as browsing the Internet, e-mail, social networking, photos, videos, games, music, radio and TV. The small size of the smartphone makes it ideal for computing on the move, including using the Internet over a cell phone network where there is no Wi-Fi.

- For some people the smartphone will meet all of their computing needs. For others it may be necessary to have laptop or desktop computers for heavyweight office-type work, while using a smartphone for the activities listed above.

Contracts and Deals

Introduction

Listed below are some of the ways to equip yourself with a new Android smartphone and connect it to a cell phone network to make phone calls, send text messages and use *data*.

- A *contract* with a network such as EE, O2, Vodafone or Three, typically for one or two years. *Upfront* and monthly payments cover the cost of a new *smartphone* and your *calls*, *texts* and *data*.

- A *"SIM-free"* smartphone can be bought separately. Then buy and insert a *SIM card* for a network of your choice.

- A *SIM-only* card can be inserted into a new or existing SIM-free smartphone and ties you to a network to which you make monthly payments.

- A *Pay As You Go* SIM card requires you to open an account with a network and keep it in credit, by topping up when necessary.

Data refers to the transfer of text, photos, Web pages, etc., during Internet activities such as E-mail, Web browsing, Facebook, streaming videos, etc.

The above topics are discussed in more detail later in this chapter.

Cell Phone Networks

These consist of towers or *base stations* sited around the country in *cells*. A cell is an area of land on which, typically, one, two or three towers are situated. The towers, also known as *transceivers*, transmit and receive wireless signals to and from your phone. The towers are connected to the public telephone network.

There are four main *host* network operators in the UK. These are EE, O2, Three and Vodafone. These companies manage their own physical networks.

Other providers of mobile phone services pay to use the four main host networks shown above and are known as *Mobile Virtual Network Operators*. Some examples are:

Virtual Network	Host Network
giffgaff	O2
BT Mobile	EE
Sky	O2
Tesco Mobile	O2
Talkmobile	Vodafone
ASDA Mobile	EE

In the remainder of this book, the term *network* will refer to both *host* and *virtual* networks.

Network Coverage

GSM (Global System for Mobile Communications) is a major mobile phone technology used in Europe and other parts of the world. Starting with 1G (first generation) networks, which could only handle phone calls, the technology developed to 2G, which added text messages and emails. Then 3G added *mobile broadband* Internet activities such as Web browsing and downloading videos.

Most areas are now provided with the latest and much faster 4G and 4G LTE network technology but a few still use the slower 3G. (5G is currently under development for introduction around 2020 onwards.)

Entering something like "**mobile network coverage UK**" into a search engine such as Google produces a list of Websites which will check the coverage in your area, for each of the popular networks. Select a network, then enter your postcode as shown below:

DG534NR	Search	See coverage for	2G	3G	**4G**

As shown above you can check for **2G**, **3G** and **4G** coverage. A coverage report for your postcode area is displayed as shown below.

4G current coverage report   ⓘ

(what is 4G?)

Indoors and outdoors, you can expect to have a reliable connection for emails and the internet using a 4G-compatible phone, laptop or tablet. You can also expect good 4G browsing and download speeds.

Live in a basement flat? You probably already know that your signal is not as good when underground.

Weak Signals

As well as a coverage report, as shown on the previous page, a colour-coded map displaying the coverage in your area is also produced, as shown below.

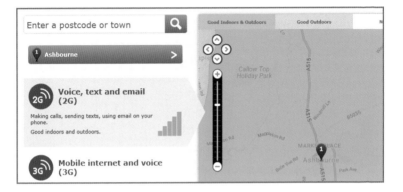

The coverage report and map may be accurate for most of an area, but there may be a few "*not-spots*" where there is no signal at all. Other locations may have weak 3G and 4G signals giving poor speeds for Internet data transfers.

Weak signals may be due to the distance of the phone from the nearest cell phone tower or obstructions such as hills, buildings, thick walls and trees.

If you have a 3G phone, it will not be able to use a 4G network, but a 4G phone can use a 3G network.

Choosing a Network

Before choosing a network, it's therefore a good idea to check the coverage in the areas where you will spend most time using your phone. Apart from the Web sites giving network coverage information mentioned above, you might also talk to friends and colleagues and also local mobile phone shops.

Purchasing Options

The main options for setting yourself up with a smartphone on a cell phone network are:

- Take out a *contract* which includes a new phone.

- Buy a *SIM card* and insert it in a new or existing phone, either on a *SIM only* network deal or as a *Pay As you Go* deal with a network.

Contracts Which Include a New Phone

Many phones are bought on a contract, usually based on 24 monthly payments. The payments cover the cost of the phone itself and all of the phone calls, text messages and data you use. With some contracts there is an upfront payment of £10-£200. If you exceed your allowance for minutes, text and data you will be billed for the excess the following month.

Networks such as Three, O2, Vodafone and EE offer a choice of smart phones including Androids from a range of manufacturers and also the rival iPhone from Apple. Shown below are the terms of a 24 month contract for the very popular Samsung Galaxy S8.

	Contract	Calls	Texts	Data	Cost
Samsung Galaxy S8 64GB FREE	24 months 4G	Unlimited minutes	Unlimited texts	5GB	**£32.99** monthly **£791.76** total

As shown above, the S8 is compatible with **4G** networks and there is no upfront payment i.e. "**FREE**". The total cost of **£791.76** pays for **Unlimited** calls, texts and **5GB** of Internet **data** as well buying the phone itself.

Data

In addition to calls in minutes and text messages, a contract will specify an allowance of, say, 5GB of *data*. (Units such as gigabytes (GB) were discussed on page 15).

This is your *data plan* and refers to Internet activities such as browsing the Web, transferring files to the Clouds, streaming music and videos and exchanging photos and messages on Facebook, Twitter and WhatsApp.

Subsidised Smartphones

To buy the Samsung Galaxy S8 *SIM-free*, i.e. on its own without a contract, currently costs £600-£700 from various retailers. To this must be added the cost of any calls, texts and data, depending on the deal you choose for the SIM-free phone (*PAYG* or a *SIM only* contract). The cost of 5GB of data over 2 years may be around £10 a month making the total cost of a SIM-free deal on the Galaxy S8 around £840-£940 over two years. The saving of perhaps £50-£150 obtained with the phone-inclusive contract deal on the previous page is possible because the cost of the phone is *subsidised* by the network provider. The contract phone is also *locked* (as discussed in Chapter 4) so it can't be used on another network until it is *unlocked*.

Using Wi-Fi (Wireless Fidelity)

It's cheaper to use Wi-Fi rather than 3G/4G for Internet activities with your smartphone. If you have a broadband network in the home and with **Wi-Fi** switched **ON** in the phone **Settings**, the phone should automatically switch to Wi-Fi for all your Internet work. You can also use Wi-Fi on your phone in hotels, cafes, airports, etc.

In places where there is no Wi-Fi, if **Mobile data** is switched **ON** in **Settings**, the phone should automatically use the phone's 3G/4G cellular network for Internet use. **Settings** are discussed later in this book.

The use of Wi-Fi is separate from your cell phone network and will not be charged to your cell phone account. Instead it will be part of your Wi-Fi broadband service with an Internet Service Provider via your telephone landline.

If using Wi-Fi in a hotel there may be a small service charge but Wi-Fi is free in many public places.

Many Wi-Fi accounts provide *unlimited data*. So, if you have access to Wi-Fi for your Internet activities, a large cell phone data allowance will not be needed — 500MB, 1GB or 2GB may be enough. This will be cheaper than a data plan of, say, 18GB a month costing £35 a month for 2 years. (This also includes payments for buying the phone).

There are lots of Web sites comparing the different networks and these can be found after entering **Cell Phone Networks** into a search engine such as Google.

For example, the **uSwitch** Website gives comprehensive details of all of the main networks. You can search for contracts for **All brands** of phone or **CHOOSE A MANUFACTURER** such as **SAMSUNG**, as shown below.

.

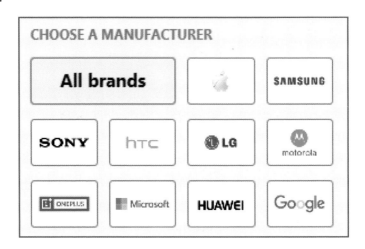

Alternatively you can view a list of contracts with **All networks** or a particular network, such as **giffgaff** shown below.

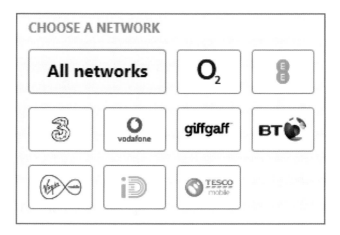

Filtering the List of Deals Displayed by uSwitch

In order to find contracts which meet your needs, you can specify the number of calls in minutes, texts and data in GB. You can also search for contracts with a specified monthly cost and a specified upfront cost.

	Available search options
Calls (minutes)	Any, 300+, 600+, 900+, Unlimited
Texts	Any, 300+, 600+, 900+, Unlimited
Data (GB)	Any, 1, 2, 3, 5, 10, 15, 20, 30, 40, Unlimited
Monthly cost (£)	Any, 10, 20, 30, 40, 50, 60, 70
Upfront cost (£)	Any, Free phone, 50, 100, 150, 200

Low Data Contracts

Shown below are two of the contracts found after a search on uSwitch for HTC and Motorola phones with a maximum monthly payment of £20.

	Contract	Calls	Texts	Data	Cost
Motorola G5 16GB	24 months 4G	Unlimited minutes	Unlimited texts	1GB data	£17.90 monthly £431.76 total
HTC One A9 16GB	24 months 4G	300 minutes	5000 texts	500MB data	£15.99 monthly £383.76 total

500MB and **1GB** data above are light data usage, e.g. for Web browsing and e-mailing for about an hour a day.

High Data Contracts

By increasing the maximum monthly payment in the uSwitch contract search to £50, the data allowance increases significantly, as shown in the two examples below. Watching a 2 hour movie can use 2-4GB of data. Most people wouldn't need 40GB of data a month unless they spent a lot of time watching videos and playing games.

	Contract	Calls	Texts	Data	Cost
HTC 10 32GB	24 months 4G	Unlimited minutes	Unlimited texts	Unlimited data	£49.00 monthly £1176.00 total
Motorola Moto G5 Plus 32GB	24 months 4G	Unlimited minutes	Unlimited texts	40GB data	£39.00 monthly £936.00 total

How Much Data Do You Need?

Research has shown that many people taking out contracts are paying for more data than they need. When you first take out a contract you need to decide how much data you require.

The most popular data allowances on contracts are 500MB, 1GB, 2GB and 5GB. As mentioned earlier, if most of your Internet activities are carried out using Wi-Fi in the home, etc., 500MB or 1GB may be enough. If you want to watch a lot of videos, stream music and play online games, a data allowance of several GB or more may be needed.

Data Rollover for Unused Data

If you have a 5GB data allowance and only use, say, 3 GB, some networks, such as Vodafone, O2, Virgin Media, Sky Mobile and iD Mobile, will "*roll over*" the unused 2 GB allowance to the next month, when you will then have 7GB. It's a good idea to check with networks to see what happens to unused data. With some deals it may be a case of "Use it or lose it!" Also some networks suspend your service and your number if the phone isn't used for 6 months.

Exceeding Your Data Allowance

If you use more data than your monthly allowance, you will be charged for the excess, perhaps £2-£3 per MB of excess data.

Setting a Data Cap

However, if you are worried about exceeding your data allowance you can set a *data cap* to limit your data usage. Network's such as Vodafone allow you to set a data cap on your account on their Website.

SIM-only Contracts

If you already have a phone that you're happy with or wish to buy a phone of your choice separately, the SIM-only contract may be a cheaper option. You will still pay monthly instalments, usually by direct debit, for your calls, texts and data but your payments don't include the cost of the phone. As discussed on page 18, *Multi SIM cards* are usually supplied and can easily be converted, if necessary, to cover any of the three sizes of SIM, i.e. *Standard*, *Micro* and *Nano*. As shown in the deals below, SIM-only deals usually involve 1 month or 12 month contracts.

Cost	Contract	Calls	Texts	Data
£4.99 monthly	**1 month 4G**	**1250 minutes**	**1250 texts**	**1.25 GB data**
£20.00 monthly	**12 months 4G**	**Unlimited minutes**	**Unlimited texts**	**10GB data**

You can view the SIM-only deals on any of the comparison Web sites, such as uSwitch.com. You can filter the deals by selecting your required network, calls, text, data and monthly payments as discussed on page 30 for the phone-inclusive contract. However, with the SIM-only deal, since you obtain the phone separately, the options to specify an upfront payment and a manufacturer do not apply.

With the 1 month or 30-day contract, you pay the fee by direct debit every month, but are free to cancel it with 30 days notice, unlike the 24 month phone-inclusive contract SIM-only deals are becoming increasingly popular as you have more freedom to change network and may be much cheaper, especially if you already have a SIM-free, *unlocked* phone. Locked and unlocked phones are discussed in Chapter 4.

PAYG (Pay As You Go)

This requires you to have a SIM-free, unlocked smartphone. Then insert a PAYG SIM card for a network of your choice. This can be obtained online or at a local shop, typically free or about £1. Apart from a Multi SIM card, the package usually includes a *top up swipe card*.

Next you need to call the network provider, register the phone in your name and top up with, say, £10 or £20 by debit or credit card. After using the phone for a while the user "tops up" their account when it's necessary.

There are various ways to top up, such as:

- Calling or texting the network provider.

- Paying a shop to put credit onto your swipe card.

- Using a menu option on a bank cashpoint/ATM.

- Using the Website of your network provider.

If you use all your credit, you will not be able to use the phone until it's topped up.

Data Packs

These are bundles of calls, text and data which last 30 days or sometimes 7 days. The payment is taken from your PAYG top up account each month.

Cost	Deal	Calls	Texts	Data
£5.00 monthly	1 month 4G	50 minutes	250 texts	150MB data
£10.00 monthly	1 month 4G	250 minutes	Unlimited texts	1GB data

Choosing a Contract or Deal

The next two pages list some of the important considerations when selecting a contract or deal for a smartphone:

- The network you choose should have good coverage, i.e. a strong signal in the places where you spend a lot of time on the phone.

- If you will be mainly using your phone where there is access to Wi-Fi, this should be switched on (as discussed in Chapter 4) and used for the Internet rather than using the 3G/4G phone network.

- Similarly you can use services such as WhatsApp and Skype to make *free* phone calls and send text messages across the Internet, so a contract with high allowances for calls and text will not be necessary.

- Unless you spend a lot of time watching videos, downloading music and playing online games where there is no Wi-Fi, you shouldn't need a contract with a large amount of data — 500MB to 3GB might be adequate. If you don't use all of your monthly allowance, some networks allow you to *roll over* your unused data and use it in the following month.

- If you exceed your monthly allowance for calls, texts and data you may be charged the following month.

- Some networks allow you to set a *data cap* to limit the amount of data you can use.

- Contracts are often for 24 monthly payments covering the cost of the phone and calls, text and messages. An upfront payment of £10 to £200 may be required.

- Some contracts tie you to the same network and phone for 2 years. A *termination fee* may be payable if you end the contract early.

- A phone bought as part of a contract is usually *locked* and must be *unlocked* to use with another network.

- The *SIM only* deal requires you to buy a SIM card for a network and insert it into an *unlocked SIM free* phone. The contracts are usually for 1 month or a year and allow more freedom than a 2 year contract.

- In a *Pay As You Go* (*PAYG*) deal you also buy a SIM card for a network and insert it into an unlocked phone. You pay in advance to add credit to your account and *top up* when required.

- *Data packs* take money from your PAYG credit to pay for "bundles" of minutes, texts and data.

- If you run out of credit on PAYG, you won't be able to use the phone, except for "emergency calls only".

- Comparison Websites like uSwitch allow you to find phone contracts or deals which meet your needs, such as your required data allowance, monthly payment, network provider and make of phone.

Related topics such tracing a *lost* or *stolen* phone, *data roaming* and checking and limiting your *data usage* are discussed in more detail in Chapter 14.

Setting Up an Android Smartphone

Introduction

There are two main processes needed to set up an Android phone for use on both Wi-Fi broadband networks and 3G/4G cell phone networks. The two processes are:

- Setting up the main Google services and your personal preferences using the Setup Wizard.
- If necessary, inserting and *activating* the SIM card which connects your phone to a cell phone network such as EE, Three, O2 and Vodafone, etc.

This chapter covers the Setup Wizard, which needs to be completed on all new Android smartphones (and tablets).

In addition to the Setup Wizard, SIM-free phones will also need a SIM card to be inserted. This can be done before or after completing the Setup Wizard. Inserting and activating a SIM card is discussed in Chapter 5.

SIM cards are pre-installed on phones bought on 12 or 24 month network contracts from a shop or online. If you later want to switch a contract phone to a new network, the phone may need to be *unlocked* as discussed on page 58. Then insert a SIM card for the new network.

The Setup Wizard tailors the phone to your requirements and is basically the same on all Android devices. The main steps are:

- Select the language you wish to use.

- Connect the phone to your Wi-Fi network.

- Create a new Google account or enter an e-mail address and password for an existing account.

- Choose various options such as backing up your data and using your location in various apps.

- Set the time and date.

- Set optional start-up security options for unlocking the screen, such as a *PIN* number, a *pattern*, *swiping* the screen or *fingerprint recognition*.

At the end of the wizard a contract phone with the SIM card pre-installed should be ready to use.

On PAYG phones, before you can use 3G/4G to make phone calls, send text messages and use the Internet where there is no Wi-Fi, you will need to insert the SIM card and *top up*, i.e. add credit to your account with a network such as EE, O2, Three, etc., as discussed in Chapter 5.

If you complete the Setup Wizard on a PAYG SIM-free phone but don't install a SIM card, you will only be able to use the phone over Wi-Fi to browse the Web, share photographs, send e-mails and watch videos, etc. You can get apps to use an Android phone without a SIM card to make calls and send messages over Wi-Fi. The Wi-Fi approach is cheaper than using a phone network but can only be used when you are connected to a Wi-Fi network, either at home or in a café, hotel or other public place.

Starting the Android Setup Wizard

In this example, a Moto G5 phone running Android 7 Nougat has been used. Nougat is the version of Android which is most widely available at the time of writing.

Make sure the phone's battery is fully charged. Then switch the phone On by holding down the **Power Button** shown on page 19. Then select a language, such as **English**, from the drop-down menu on the **Welcome** screen, shown below.

Select **GET STARTED** and you can then choose from the two options shown on the next page.

As you progress through the steps of the wizard, you may need to tap **NEXT** to move on to the next step. Alternatively you may have the option to **Skip** a setting. In this case you can return to a setting later using the Android **Settings** feature discussed later in this book.

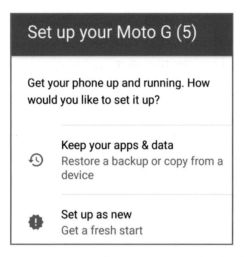

Keep your apps & data above recovers backed up files or copies files from a previous device. This recovery will require an existing Google user name and password.

Select **Set up as new** as shown above and you can connect to the Internet after selecting a local Wi-Fi network detected by your phone, typically the *broadband router* in your home or in a hotel, etc., such as **BTHub5-9CHT** below.

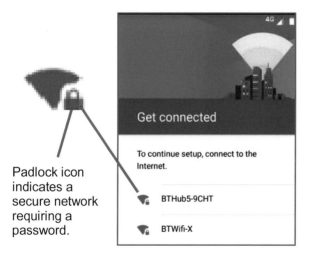

Padlock icon indicates a secure network requiring a password.

Select your network from the list shown on the previous page, then, if necessary, enter the password, usually found on the back of the network router.

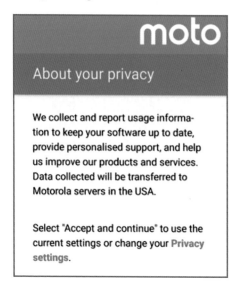

After entering the password for the network and selecting **CONNECT** shown above, the connection to the Wi-FI router is made. You are then asked to **Accept and continue** or **change your Privacy settings** as shown below.

The **Add your account** screen appears, allowing you to sign in with an **Email or phone** number for an existing Google account **Or create a new account**.

The Google Account

All Android operating systems, such as Marshmallow, Nougat and Oreo are products of Google LLC. If you select to **create a new account** shown above, you will switch on many important Google features, such as:

- Data such as e-mails, contacts, files, etc., will be *synced* and accessible on multiple devices, such as Android phones, tablets and Windows computers.

- Your data will be backed up automatically to the clouds so that it can be restored to another device if your phone is lost or stolen.

- You can access the Google Play Store for the downloading of apps, in addition to those apps already installed on a new Android phone.

A Google account is needed to make the most of a wide range of useful Google apps and services on Android phones, including those shown below:

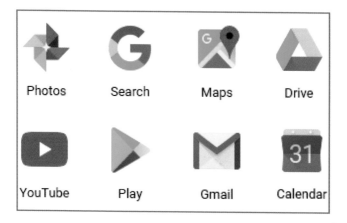

If you choose to **SKIP** the creation of a Google account, as shown at the bottom of the **Add your account** window on page 42, the Google apps and their icons shown above will still appear on your Apps screen, but you will not be able to use them straightaway.

Instead the **Add your account** window shown on page 42 appears, requiring you to create a new Google account in order to use the Google apps and services shown above.

Creating a Google Account

To create a new Google account, you are asked to enter your first name, last name, date of birth and gender before entering a username such as:

johnbrown@gmail.com

(**@gmail.com** is already entered)

Then enter and confirm a strong password as a mixture of numbers, letters and symbols.

After tapping **ACCEPT** to agree to the **Terms of Service** and **Privacy Policy**, you can add to your Google account the number of the phone you're currently setting up.

This will be used across Google services, for example to reset your password if you forget it or to receive video calls and text messages. Select **YES, I'M IN** shown above to continue. Next you are asked to read through Google's Privacy and Terms before selecting **I accept** to create your account.

You can then choose to accept or switch off a large number of Google services, such as those shown in the small sample below.

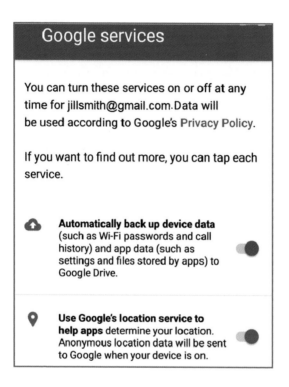

Next you can select **Add fingerprint** as shown on the next page, if you wish to use the *fingerprint sensor* shown on page 19 to unlock the *Lock Screen*. The Lock Screen appears when the phone is first switched on or when it's woken from a period of sleep or inactivity.

To set up fingerprint recognition you are asked to tap your finger several times on the sensor at the bottom of the screen.

If you choose to **Skip** a setting, as shown above, you can return to it later in the main Android **Settings** feature, discussed later.

Lock Screen vs Locked Phone

Methods of locking and unlocking the *Lock Screen*, such as fingerprint recognition shown above, are security features used to stop someone else using your phone.

Conversely, a *locked phone* is one tied by software to a particular network, such as EE, O2, Three or Vodafone. A locked phone must first be *unlocked* before it can be used on a different network, as discussed in Chapter 5.

Finally there are some optional settings such as your payment method for Google products from the Play Store and *voice recognition* for searching, etc.

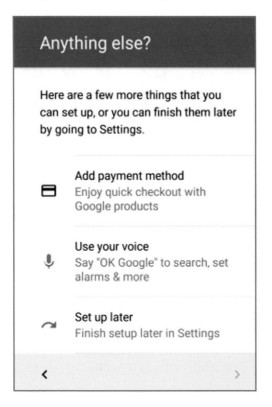

That completes most of the settings on a new or factory reset ("wiped") phone. As mentioned elsewhere, you can make changes to the settings at any time after tapping the **Settings** button shown on the right.

The **Settings** feature is discussed in more detail later in this book.

At the end of the setting up process, your phone will display the Home and Apps screens with the pre-installed apps as shown below.

Home Screen   **Apps Screen**

Activating an Android Phone

If you've bought a phone on a 12 or 24 month contract it should be ready to use on Wi-Fi and 3G/4G after the Setup Wizard just described in this chapter.

As mentioned earlier you can insert a SIM card in a PAYG phone either before or after completing the Setup Wizard. Either way, the SIM card will need to be *topped up* with credit and *activated* before the phone can be used to make phone calls, send text messages and use *mobile data* to access the Internet across a 3G/4G cell phone network

Inserting and activating a SIM Card for use on a 3G/4G cell phone network is discussed in detail in the next chapter.

Inserting and Activating a SIM Card

Introduction

As discussed earlier, there are several ways to equip yourself with an Android smartphone. These include:

- Buying a new phone on a contract, typically 12 or 24 months. This may involve a credit check.

- Buying a new SIM-free phone and inserting a SIM card for a network of your choice. (Either on a SIM-only contract or PAYG).

Contract Phone

If you buy a phone from a network such as EE, etc., the SIM card should have been pre-installed. You set up your contract and direct debit details with the network either in a shop or online. After completing the Setup Wizard (described in Chapter 4) the phone should be ready to use.

SIM-free Phone

With a SIM-free phone you will need to complete the Setup Wizard and *install* and *activate* the SIM card. It doesn't matter whether you install the SIM card before or after completing the Setup Wizard. However, you can't activate and start using the phone on a network such as Three, O2 or Vodafone until the wizard is completed.

Inserting a SIM Card

As discussed on page 18, there are 3 sizes of SIM card, Standard, Micro and Nano. Most SIM cards are supplied as part of a triple pack containing one of each size of card.

If necessary, remove the surrounding material to obtain a SIM card to suit the slot size in your phone. The slot for the SIM card may be on the outside of the phone, enabling the card to be easily inserted and removed.

Alternatively the SIM card slot may be inside the phone, next to the battery, as shown below.

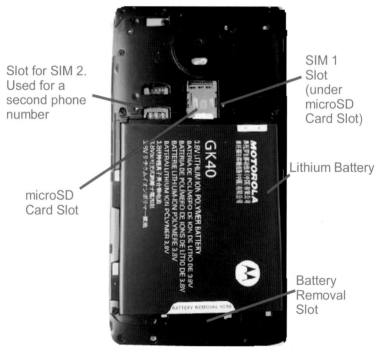

Slot for SIM 2. Used for a second phone number

SIM 1 Slot (under microSD Card Slot)

Lithium Battery

microSD Card Slot

Battery Removal Slot

SIM Card Slots in the Motorola Moto G5

For a phone with an internal SIM card slot, with the phone switched off, remove the back cover to reveal the SIM card slot as shown on the previous page. Then carefully remove the battery using a finger or plastic lever in the battery removal slot shown on the previous page.

Make sure your new SIM is the correct size for the slot, as discussed on page 18. The new SIM card should be gently pushed into the slot in the phone. There may be a small diagram on the phone, as shown for **SIM 2** below, to show which way the SIM is to be inserted, relative to the card's cutaway corner.

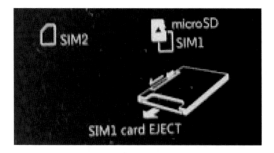

In the case of an internal SIM card, replace the battery and back cover. You may need to charge the battery before switching on.

Dual SIM Cards

Some smartphones have a second SIM slot, so that you can use the phone with two separate phone numbers, as shown in the Moto G5 on page 50.

microSD Card

A slot for a *microSD card* is also built into some phones, to supplement the internal storage. In the Moto G5 a microSD card up to 256GB can be inserted in a slot above the **SIM1** slot as shown above and on page 50.

Activating a SIM Card

At the end of the setup process, your phone will display the Home and Apps screens as shown on page 48. Shown below is part of the Home screen with the *Navigation Bar* along the bottom and the *Favorites Tray* above it. The various screens and icons are discussed in more detail in Chapter 9.

As shown on page 48, the phone icon appears on both the Home and Apps screens.

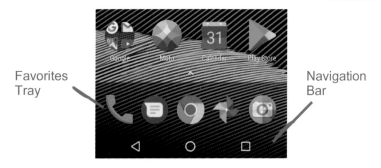

Favorites
Tray

Navigation
Bar

If you've bought a phone on a 12 or 24 month contract it should be ready to use after the general Android setup procedure described in Chapter 4.

If you've set up a PAYG phone with a new SIM card it needs to be topped up and may need to be *activated* so that it can be used to make phone calls, send text messages and use *mobile data* across a 3G/4G cell phone network.

Some networks supply SIM cards which are *pre-activated* which means activation is automatic. In some cases, activation may be immediate, may take a few seconds but in other cases may take up to 24 hours.

If a SIM is activated the network name such as EE and the triangular icon shown on the right should appear on the screen.

Topping up may involve one or more of the following:

- Visiting the network's activation Web page and:

   Entering an *activation code* supplied on the SIM card instructions or packaging then entering your bank account details.

   Or entering a number from a top-up voucher bought from a shop, or other outlet displaying the green top-up sign.

- Making a phone call to a number provided by the network, then following the resulting voice mail instructions from the network.

- Making a phone call to any number of your choice and following the resulting voice mail instructions.

During the top-up process you may be asked to provide the following numbers:

SIM Card Number

19 or 20 characters stored on the card. Can be found in **Settings/About phone/Status/SIM status**.

IMEI Number

15 digits on the box the phone came in or in **Settings/About phone/Status/IMEI information**. Or dial ***#06#** on the phone you are activating.

Your Phone Number

Mobile phone number found in **Settings/About phone/ Status/SIM status/My phone number**.

Topping Up a Pay As You Go SIM Card

Full instructions for topping up are usually given in the SIM card package. A variety of methods of topping up, as discussed on the previous page, are available on the networks such as EE, O2, Vodafone and Three. Each network usually offers several alternative methods of topping up. A few examples are given below:

EE

Tap the blue phone icon on your Apps Screen or on the Home Screen.

- Tap the keypad icon shown on the right.
- Enter any genuine phone number to dial, then tap the green phone icon on the keypad.

Then a voice mail message gives you the following options:

Press 1: Top up now with a credit card.

Press 2: Send a free "call me back" text to the person you're trying to contact.

Top up using one of the following:

- Online at the My EE Website.
- At a bank cashpoint.
- At an EE Store.
- By sending a text message.
- At shops, post offices, etc., wherever you see the green top-up sign, shown on the right, using a top-up card.

Three

Buy a Three top-up voucher from a local shop or have your credit or debit card ready. Go to **Top-up Three** on **www.three.co.uk**, then scroll down and select **Top-up now**.

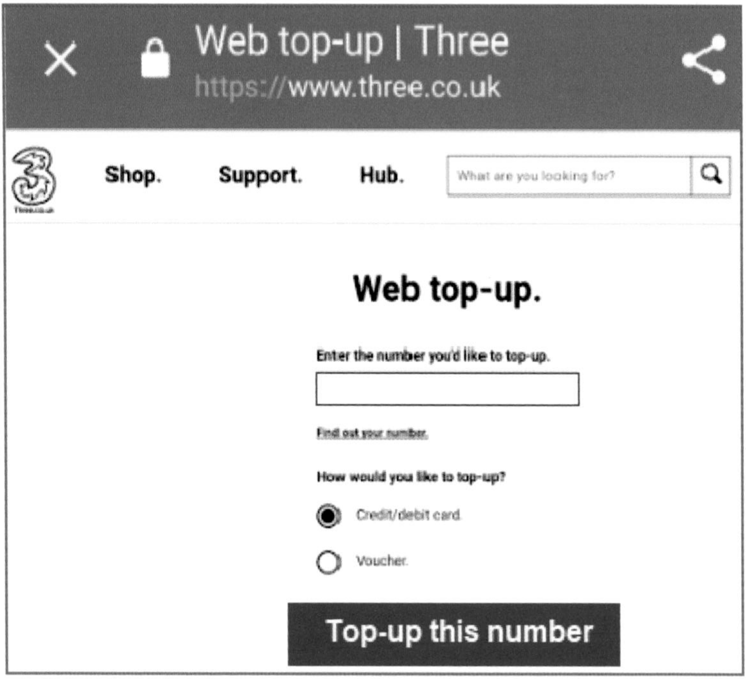

Enter in the box shown above, the number of the phone you're topping up, found as discussed on page 53.

- Select either **Credit/debit card** or **Voucher** shown above.

- Select the amount you wish to top up by, from £10 to £50.

- Enter your bank details or the 16-digit voucher number.

Vodafone

After inserting a new SIM card, Vodafone ask you to activate and top up using a choice of methods, similar to those discussed on the previous two pages .

Activate your SIM card

1. Put your SIM in your phone.

2. Call **17298** for free from your Vodafone mobile.

Top up your new SIM card

1. Call **2345** for free from your Vodafone mobile

2. Top up direct from your bank account.

3. Top up through My Vodafone.

4. Buy a top up voucher at over 150,000 cashpoints or retailers.

My Vodafone highlighted above is a free app, downloadable from the Play Store which allows you to make instant top ups and track your spending.

My Vodafone
Vodafone UK Limited

O2

Various plans or "goodybags"are available from £10 to £20 for various amounts of data, calls in minutes and texts. The procedure for topping up O2 is as follows:

- Call **4444** free or visit **O2.co.uk/topup**.
- Top up with at least £10 to get the Big Bundle.

giffgaff

giffgaff is a virtual network, hosted by O2 and specialising in non-contract, PAYG packages. The giffgaff SIM card is enclosed in a package containing a lot of helpful instructions for activation, as shown below.

> **1.** Go to **giffgaff.com/activate** and enter the code on the back of your SIM card.
>
> **2.** Have your credit/debit card or top-up voucher to hand and follow the instructions.
>
> **3.** Pop your SIM into an unlocked phone, check **giffgaff.com/unlock** for help.
>
> ✓ Job done. You're now a fully fledged giffgaff member. Welcome.

Activation Time

After topping up, activation (if not already pre-activated) is usually very quick although on some networks may take up to 24 hours. Once activated you can use the phone for calls, text messages and Internet activities over your chosen 3G/4G cell network, wherever there is a phone signal.

Mobile Data

To use the Internet over a 3G/4G phone network, in places where there is no Wi-Fi, **Mobile data** must be is switched **On** in **Settings/Data/Usage** or in **Settings**/**SIM cards/Mobile data** as shown below

Settings

Mobile data

SIM1: 3 UK

Previously Used Phones

Unlocking a Phone

If a phone has been previously bought on a contract with a network it may need to be *unlocked* before you can insert a new SIM card for another network.

A network can use a software code to *lock* a phone, preventing it from being used on any other network. To use the phone on a new network, you need to ask your old network to *unlock* it. An unlocking fee, typically up to about £20 may be charged. It may not be possible to unlock a phone until you've fulfilled your contract.

Local mobile phone shops also offer unlocking services.

Keeping the Same Phone Number

If moving to a new network, via a new SIM or a new phone, it might be a big task to inform all of your contacts of the your new phone number. You would probably need to send a lot of text messages to your doctor, dentist, etc. Ask your old network for a *PAC* (*Porting Authorisation Code*). This is usually 9 digits long and lasts for 30 days. Give the code to the new network provider who will use it to transfer your old number to your phone on the new network.

Moving a SIM card to Another Phone

If you buy a new phone and insert your old SIM card, you will still be on the same network and have the same phone number. Contacts are automatically *synced* or copied to a new phone if you sign in with the same *Google account* i.e. username and password, on both old and new phones.

Removing a SIM Card

There may be small lever on an internal SIM card slot, as shown below.

On an external SIM card slot, use a finger or paper clip, etc.

Bundles

As part of the process of setting up a new PAYG SIM card, you may be offered a choice of *bundles* or *packs*. The PAYG SIM card for a network may offer a choice of data plans of minutes, texts and data, typically costing in the range £5 to £30 as shown below and on page 34. These are flexible, i.e. you can change the plan each month or 30 days in some cases. They may also offer *rollover*, so that you only pay for what you use. Any unused allowances of minutes, texts and data are carried over to the next month. The bundle may renew automatically as long as there is enough credit in your account. The examples below are the cheapest and dearest bundles offered with a free SIM card from a major network and include rollover.

Top Up	Data	Minutes	Texts
£5	100MB	100	250
£30	20GB	3000	Unlimited

SIM Card vs Wi-Fi

- The SIM card (*Subscriber Identity Module*) connects your phone to the *towers* of a 3G/4G cell phone network such as EE, Vodafone, Three and O2.

- The SIM card enables calls, texts and Internet over 3G/4G. Using the Internet over 3G/4G is more expensive than over Wi-Fi.

- If you are connected simultaneously to both 3G/4G and Wi-Fi, an Android device will automatically use the much cheaper Wi-Fi connection to the Internet.

- Wi-Fi is used by your phone to access the Internet via a *router* connected to the BT telephone lines or a *fibre-optic* cable network. You need to be within the *range* of the router, which may be about 50m-100m.

- Wi-Fi is available in the home and in places such as cafes, hotels, buses, airports, etc., and is often free.

- Some cell phone networks are now introducing *Wi-Fi calling* on *compatible* phones. Wi-Fi calls via a cell phone network are still charged at normal rates but are advantageous where there are weak 3G/4G signals.

- A phone with Wi-Fi but without a SIM card for a network can still be used for a wide range of free Internet and other activities.

- WhatsApp, a free app from the Google Play Store, provides free calls and messaging over Wi-Fi. WhatsApp can also use your 3G/4G Internet connection for calls and messages and this may result in a charge against your data plan.

- However, if you need to use your phone on the move, in places where there is no Wi-Fi, then a phone with a 3G/4G SIM card for a cell phone network is essential.

Phone Calls and Contacts

Introduction

The mobile phone has evolved over the last few decades as follows:

1st Generation

1G cell phones were produced in the 1980s and could only be used for voice calls.

2nd Generation

2G phones followed in the early 1990s and introduced *SMS* (Short Messaging Service) for text-only messages. 2G also included *MMS* (Multimedia Messaging Service) which allows pictures and videos to be sent with messages.

3rd Generation

Developed in the years 2001-2007, 3G brought *mobile data* services so the phone could be used for Internet activities such as Web browsing and e-mail, etc.

4th Generation

First launched in 2012, 4G provides access to the full range of Internet activities – like 3G but up to 10 times faster.

This chapter covers making and receiving voice only phone calls. Chapter 7 describes the use of the phone for SMS and MMS messages.

Chapters 8-14 cover the use of an Android phone as a *tablet computer* for Internet activities such as Web browsing, e-mail, social networking and the sharing of photos using either Wi-Fi or mobile data.

Finding Your New Phone Number

You will need your new phone number handy when other people ask for it. There are a several ways to find it:

- Select the Android **Settings** icon shown on the right, followed by **About phone** then **Status** and **SIM status.** Then your number is displayed under **My phone number**.

Settings

- Or, on some versions of Android, select the **Settings** icon and then select **SIM cards** to display your phone number as shown below.

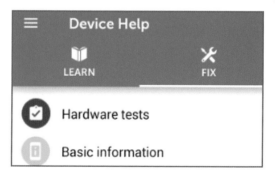

- Or, from the **Apps** screen, select the **Device Help** icon shown on the right then select **FIX** followed by **Basic information**.

Device Help

- Or call a nearby phone and read your number from the call **Log** on that phone.

Making a Call

This section describes making a basic call using the default ringtone and blank facial image. (Personalising **Contacts** is discussed shortly.)

- Switch on the phone by holding down the **Power Button**, as shown on page 19.

- If necessary, unlock the startup **Lock Screen** using one of the following: **Swipe**, **PIN**, **Pattern**, **Password** or **Fingerprint** scanning. (See pages 46 and 175).

- Tap the phone icon on the **Home** screen or **Apps** screen.

Marshmallow, Nougat   TouchWiz

- The **Phone** app opens on the screen as shown on the next page. There are 4 main **Phone** screens, accessed by the icons shown below.

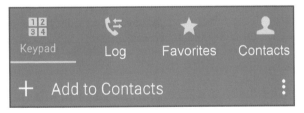

- Whenever you select the **Phone** icon, the **Phone** app opens displaying the last used screen, **Keypad**, **Log**, **Favorites** or **Contacts**.

Please note: This book has been prepared using both the "stock" or standard version of Android and the Samsung TouchWiz version. Screenshots of both versions of Android have been included where necessary.

The screenshot on the previous page were taken from a Samsung phone. Other Android phones are basically the same but may have slightly different icons and colours, as shown in the Moto G5 screenshots below. This is the *stock*, "untweaked", i.e. standard version of Android.

Favorites   Log   Contacts   Keypad

- Type in a phone number using the keypad as shown below and tap the central green phone icon at the bottom of the screen.

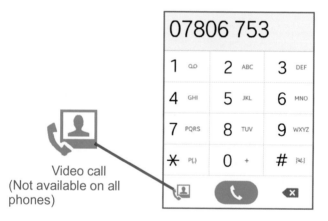

Video call
(Not available on all
phones)

- The dialling screen appears showing the number you are calling. The red phone icon at the bottom of the screen, shown here on the right, allows you to prematurely halt the call.

Accepting or Rejecting a Call

There are some alternative ways to accept a call:

- The person receiving a call on a Samsung phone can slide the green icon to the right to accept the call or slide the red icon to the left to reject it.

- On stock Androids, if you are not running an app when a call is received, a phone icon appears within flashing circles of dots as shown below. Slide the icon right to accept or left to reject

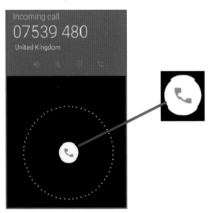

- If you are running an app when the call is received, the **ANSWER** or **REJECT** options appear at the top of the screen as shown below.

07539 480
Incoming call

REJECT   ANSWER

During a Call

While you are in a conversation, the icons shown below, appear on the screen.

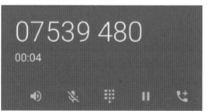

End call

 The *speakerphone* lets other people nearby, in the same room, hear the conversation.

 The *mute* icon switches off your microphone so the caller can't hear you but you can still hear them.

 Opens the *keypad*, as shown on page 64, sometimes needed during a voice call.

 Puts the call on *hold* until you tap hold again.

Add another person to the conversation to create a *conference call*.

On the TouchWiz user interface the icons appear in the format shown below, but are otherwise very similar.

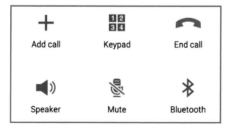

Managing Your Contacts

The previous section showed the basic method of dialling and accepting a call after entering someone's number in the keypad. This section shows how you can build up a **Contacts** list to store the numbers and personal details of the people you need to call. This makes it easy to call someone without keying in their number every time. You can also include their photograph and a personal ringtone so you'll know who's calling you.

There are several ways to create a contact, as discussed below.

- Touch the phone icon, as shown in the two examples below, on your **Home** or **Apps** screen.

Marshmallow, Nougat

TouchWiz

- The **Phone** screen opens. Now, if necessary, tap the icon shown on the right to open the **Contacts** screen shown below.

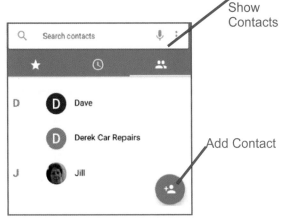

Show Contacts

Add Contact

The TouchWiz **Contacts** screen has the same features but a slightly different design.

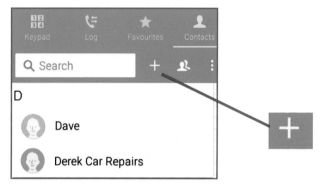

Adding a New Contact

- Tap the **Add new contact** icon shown below and on the **Contacts** screen as shown above and at the bottom of page 67.

- The buttons shown below can also be used to launch the new contact screens, shown on the next page. The buttons appear when you dial someone not yet in your **Contacts** list. Also when you tap a name in your call **Log** of a person who is not in your **Contacts** list.

- This opens the **Add new contact** screen ready for you to start entering their personal details, such as their name, phone numbers, address, e-mail address and birthday, as shown on the next page.

Including a Photograph

- Tap the camera or photo icon shown on the right above.

- You can then choose to take a photo with your phone's camera or retrieve one from the storage on your phone. (You can also change an existing photo.)

Change photo
Take photo
Choose photo

- Instead of a blank image, the photograph shows straightaway who's calling you, as shown below.

Dialling Your Contacts

This saves entering the phone number every time you call someone.

- Open your **Contacts** screen, shown below, from the **Phone** screen, as discussed on page 67 or tap the **Contacts** icon on the **Apps** screen, as shown below.

Marshmallow, Nougat

TouchWiz

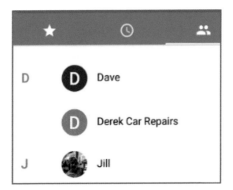

- To call (or text) one of your **Contacts**, select their name and then tap the small phone icon (or text icon) that appears against their number, as shown below.

Text message

Voice call

Finding Contacts Quickly Using the Keypad

- With the **Keypad** selected as shown on page 64, start entering your contact's number. As you enter the first few numbers, such as **07** shown below, a list of all the contacts starting with those numbers is displayed. Tap the contact to start dialling.

- Groups of 3 letters appear beneath or at the side of the numbers on the keypad. If, for example, you tap the number **5**, a list of all your contacts starting with **J**, **K** or **L** will appear after you tap the arrow under the **7** shown on the right and below.

7 contacts found starting with J,K, or L. Tap to see them.

- Tap the required contact from the list shown in the extract on the right above to start dialling the contact.

The Call Log

This lists all of the calls you've made and received and also any calls you have missed or rejected. The TouchWiz call **Log** is shown below.

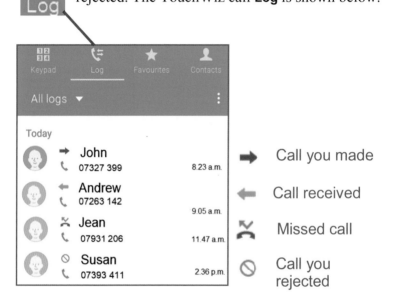

The stock Android call **Log** is similar with green arrows to represent incoming and outgoing calls and red arrows for missed calls.

- Tap on the entry in the **Call Log** to return the call, view the call details or send a text message. Text messages are discussed shortly.

Favorites

When you open the **Phone** screen, the **Favorites** icon appears on the top, as shown in the examples below. Tapping this icon shows the people you contact most often. To call someone just tap their entry in **Favorites**.

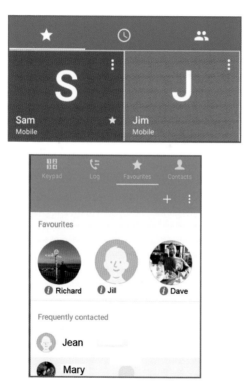

To add a contact to **Favorites**, select them in **Contacts** and then tap the star icon.

Editing a Contact

- Open the **Contacts** screen as discussed by tapping the **Phone** and **Contacts** icons as shown on page 67. Then select the person whose details you wish to edit. The screen opens with three icons as shown below on the top right.

- Tap the 3-dot menu button shown on the right and above to display the options shown below. **Share** allows you to send the details of the contact to destinations via Gmail, text message or Google Drive, etc.

Delete

Share

Place on Home screen

Adding an Icon for a Contact

- **Place on Home screen** above adds an icon for the contact to your **Home** screen. This makes it very easy to call a regular contact or edit their details.

- Tap the pencil icon shown on the right and on page 74. The **Edit contact** screen opens as shown below. This allows you to update or amend any of your contact's personal details such as their phone number or address.

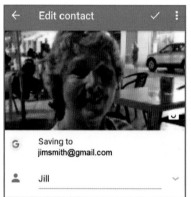

- Tap the 3-dot menu button shown on the right and above to open the menu shown below.

Delete

Set ringtone

All calls to voicemail ☐

- Switch **All calls to voice mail** on with a tick by tapping in the square if you don't want to speak to this contact. Then they can only send you voice mail messages.

Setting a Ringtone

This option allows you to set distinctive ringtones for selected contacts so you can tell straightaway when they're calling you. If you don't set any ringtones, the default ringtone will be used for all of your incoming calls.

- From the **Edit contact** screen shown on page 75, tap the 3-dot menu button shown again on the right. On TouchWiz tap the pencil icon.

- Tap **Set ringtone**, as shown on the menu at the bottom of page 75. On TouchWiz tap **Ringtone**. The list of ringtones appears, as shown in part below.

Ringtones
⦿ Bird Loop
◯ Brilliant_Times
◯ Chimey Phone
◯ Complex
CANCEL   OK

- Tap a ringtone to hear a sample.
- Scroll up or down to see many more ringtones.
- With your chosen ringtone selected, tap **OK**.
- Finally tap the tick shown below and on page 75 to finish editing and save the amended contact. On TouchWiz tap **SAVE**.

←   **Edit contact**   ✓   ⋮

Copying Contacts to a New Phone

If you acquire a new phone, it would be a tedious job to type all of your previous contacts into it. Fortunately Android makes the copying of contacts automatic, provided you have:

1. Set up your own *Google account*.
2. **Automatic backup** switched ON in **Settings**.
3. **Sync** switched ON in **Contacts** in **Accounts**.

Your Google Account

It is recommended that you set up a Google account during the initial Android Setup Wizard on a new phone. If not, or if you want to create a new account, this can be done at any time later, as discussed on pages 42-45.

When you sign into another device, such as a new phone, *with the same username and password* for your Google account as used on your other phone, your **Contacts** and other data will automatically be *synced*, i.e. copied to the new phone.

Automatic Backup

Automatic backup saves copies of all of your data, including your **Contacts**, to *Google Drive*, the cloud storage system on the Internet.

Automatically back up device data should be switched ON, during the setting up of a new phone, as discussed on page 45. Or it can be switched ON afterwards in:

Settings

Settings / Backup and reset / Back up my data

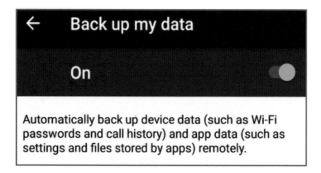

As well as **Contacts**, all of your other data, such as messages and photos, is backed up to Google Drive.

Syncing Data

Syncing copies all of your **Contacts** (and other data) from Google Drive to any other phone you sign into.

- Select **Settings / Accounts / Google** and make sure **Contacts** are set to be synced, with the **Sync** button in the ON position as shown below.

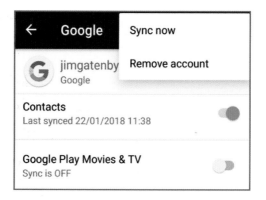

- To copy the latest data to other devices immediately, select the 3-dot menu button and then tap **Sync now**, shown above.

Sending and Receiving Text Messages

Introduction

Sending text messages or "texting" to another cell phone is one of the most popular activities with smartphones. There are two basic types of message:

SMS (Short Message Service)

A plain text message of up to 160 characters. Longer messages are divided up and sent in separate parts. Texts are normally part of your allowance with your cell phone network such as EE, Vodafone, etc. Depending on your contract or deal, SMS texts may be free.

MMS (Multi Media Messaging Service)

In addition to text, MMS messages can include photos and video and audio files as *attachments*. Unlike SMS texts, the networks may charge around 50p for an MMS message.

This can result in a heavy bill, especially if you like to send lots of *emojis* (as shown below), with your text messages.

Including a picture or image such as an emoji causes the SMS to be converted to an MMS.

Sending a Text Message

Tap the icon for the **Messages** app on the **Home** or **Apps** screen The icon appears in various formats in different versions of Android, as shown below.

Marshmallow

Nougat

TouchWiz

The **Messages** screen appears, listing any messages which have already been received. Each entry in the list represents a *conversation* with that contact, as discussed on page 86.

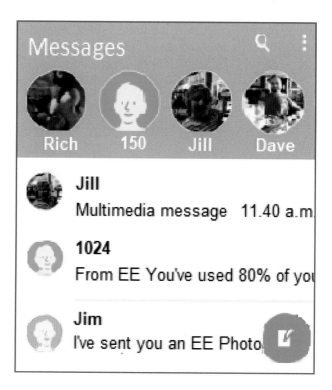

Tap the **New Message** icon, as shown on the previous page and in the examples below for different Android versions.

Marshmallow

Nougat

TouchWiz

On stock, i.e. standard Androids, the **New conversation** screen opens, as shown below. The equivalent **New message** screen on Samsung's *TouchWiz* Android user interface is shown on the next page.

Entering Recipients' Phone Numbers

Tap in the **To** bar shown on the previous page or the **Enter recipients** bar shown above and start entering a phone number. Any of your contacts whose phone number begins with those digits, such as **07** in this example, will appear as shown below.

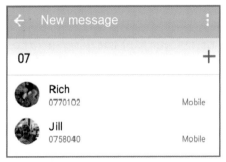

Tap the contact, such as **Rich** or **Jill** shown on the previous page, to automatically finish entering their number. If the recipient is not yet in your **Contacts** list, their phone number will need to be typed in full.

Selecting Contacts

As shown on page 81, the stock version of Android lists your **Top contacts** on the **New conversation** screen, making it easy to select them as recipients of the new message.

To text your contacts on a Samsung phone, select the icon shown on the right and on the **New Message** screen on page 82. Then select the contacts who are to receive the message and tap **DONE**.

Using the Contacts App

Select the **Contacts** app from the **Home** or **Apps** screen, as shown below.

Then select the recipient(s) from the list of contacts and tap the text icon as shown below.

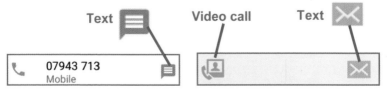

Entering the Text

Enter the recipient(s) in the **To** or **Enter recipients** bar as discussed on pages 81 and 82. In this example, **Sam** was selected from the existing **Contacts** list.

To add more recipients of the message, tap one of the icons (or similar) as shown on the right. These appear as shown above on the top right of the new message screen. After tapping the icon, choose the additional recipients from the **Contacts** as shown on page 81.

Type the message into the text bar as shown below.

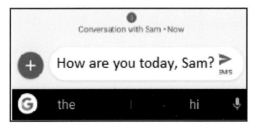

Sending the Message

After entering the text, tap the **SMS** icon, as shown on the right, to send the message to the recipient(s).

SMS

Alternatively, on Samsung TouchWiz, tap the send icon shown on the right and at the bottom right of this page.

Receiving the Message

The next time the recipient taps their **Messages** icon, they will see the new text message, as shown below.

The recipient taps the entry in their list of messages from various contacts, to see the full message and enter a reply, at the flashing cursor, as shown below.

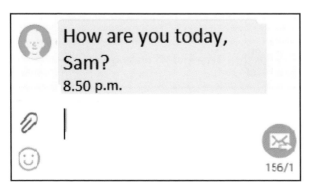

Replying to a Message

The recipient enters their reply as shown below and then taps the **SEND** icon shown on the right and below.

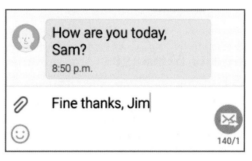

The sender of the original message receives the reply as shown below and posts another message.

Continuing this process produces a *conversation* consisting of a sequence of exchanges of texts. Each conversation with a contact can be viewed by selecting their name in the **Messages** list, shown on pages 80 and 85.

Including Attachments in a Message

Tap the *attach* icon such as those shown in the examples below. These appear next to the message entry bars shown on page 86 and elsewhere.

A variety of media can be added as attachments. The attachment screens are different in appearance for the various versions of Android but the media options are very similar, as shown below and on the next page.

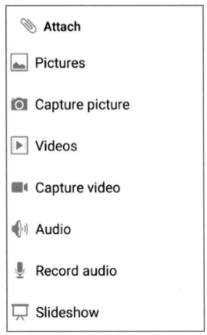

Android Marshmallow

The attachments in Android Nougat, shown below, can include emojis, animations, a map of your location and voice messages, as well as stored photos and photos taken for a message using the **Camera** app on your phone.

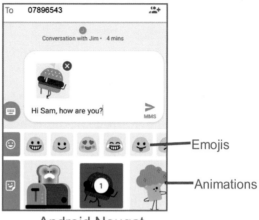

Emojis

Animations

Android Nougat

 Emojis are also available for insertion in a message after tapping the emoji key, shown on the left and on page 89, on the on-screen keyboard

The Samsung TouchWiz version of Android displays the **Attach** options on the screen, as shown below.

Including a Photo

If you choose to browse for a photo stored on your device, the image is inserted into the message, as shown below in the Marshmallow version of Android.

To send the message, tap the icon shown on the right and above. On stock Android phones, the **SEND** icon changes from **SMS** to **MMS** as shown on the right, when you include a photo, etc.

On the Samsung TouchWiz user interface the **SEND** icon, as shown on the right, is the same for both **SMS** and **MMS** messages.

The **MMS** message is received and read in the same way as an **SMS** message and a conversation can begin, as shown below, similar to the text-only conversation on page 86.

However, there are limits with different cell phone networks, as to the size of files, such as photos, videos, etc., that can be sent as attachments. This may slow or even prevent the transmission of a message

Warning! Please note:

Attaching photos, emojis, etc., will cause a simple **SMS** text message to be converted to an **MMS** message. Sending a lot of messages with emojis can result in very large bills from a cell phone network provider.

This chapter has discussed the pre-installed **Messages** app built into the stock Android operating system and also the Samsung TouchWiz user interface. Alternative messaging apps such as WhatsApp, Instagram and Snapchat are discussed later in this book.

Further Skills and Settings

Introduction

The first half of this book introduced the Android phone and its setting up. Also the basic phone functions of making and receiving voice calls and sending and receiving text messages. Until a few years ago these were the only activities possible with *mobile phones*, before the arrival of *smartphones* connected to 3G and 4G cell phone networks.

The smartphone (as opposed to the basic mobile phone) is also capable of carrying out general computing activities normally associated with larger devices such as tablet, laptop and desktop computers. These computing activities include using a phone to:

- *Browse* or search the Web for information.

- *Download* and use apps or programs for, seemingly, every conceivable purpose. Many apps are free.

- *Communicate* world-wide using email, social networking and free video calls.

- *Download* videos, music, TV and software.

- Use the *"Clouds"* to securely back up your files and make them available anywhere, on any computer.

- Use *mobile data* to connect to the Internet in places where there is no Wi-Fi.

- *Share* photos and other files with friends.

In general, as well as smartphones, much of the rest of this book also applies to Android *tablet computers*.

This chapter covers some of the further skills needed to use the Android phone for a wide range of computing and Internet activities, rather than the basic phone tasks covered earlier in this book.

Using the Touch Screen

- A single *tap* on the icon for an app opens the app on the screen.

- Tap in a text-entry slot or bar and the *on-screen keyboard* pops up ready for you to start typing.

- *Tap and hold* displays a menu relevant to the current screen.

- *Touch and hold* an item such as an icon for an app or a *widget* (discussed in Chapter 10), before dragging it to a new position with the finger.

- *Swipe* or *slide* a finger across the screen to scroll across Home Screens or unlock the Lock Screen.

Please Note:

- You might prefer to use a cheap *stylus*, as shown below, instead of your fingers, to operate the touch screen.

- Instead of entering words using the on-screen keyboard, Android has a very effective *voice recognition* system, discussed on page 118.

The On-screen Keyboard

The on-screen keyboard, shown below, pops up whenever you tap in a slot intended for the entry of text.

The On-screen Keyboard

The three icons at the bottom of the on-screen keyboard above have the following functions:

 Hide the on-screen keyboard.

 Return to the central Home Screen, discussed in Chapter 9.

 Display recently visited screens in the form of a revolving *carousel*, known as *Overview Mode*, as shown on page 109.

As shown on the next page, other versions of Android, such as Marshmallow, may have the same keyboard layout but a different colour scheme from Nougat, shown above.

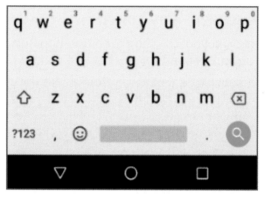

The On-screen Keyboard (Marshmallow)

Apart from letters and numbers shown above, the on-screen keyboard has the following keys:

 This toggle key is used to switch between letters, as shown above, or a combination of numbers, punctuation marks and symbols.

 The *emoji* key displays a selection of facial images to insert in the text of an email or document, etc.

 The **Shift** key is used to switch between upper and lower case letters.

 The **Backspace** key deletes letters one at a time along a line from right to left.

The **Search** key, starts a search for a keyword entered in the **Search Bar** in a program such as Google Search.

Voice Recognition

Google Docs is a wordprocessing app provided free with the Android operating system and discussed in more detail later. When entering the text in Google Docs formatting tools such as **B**old, *I*talic and Underline appear automatically on the on-screen keyboard as shown in the extract below. A *microphone* icon also appears as shown on the right and below on Android Nougat.

Tap the microphone icon and **Speak now** is displayed, as shown below. Then start entering the text by speaking, rather than typing.

Voice recognition can be used wherever you see the microphone icon, such as when searching with Google, as shown below.

Quick Settings

As discussed on pages 98 and 99, the Android operating system has a comprehensive **Settings** app used to set up and control the many functions of an Android phone. The main **Settings** app is accessed by tapping the icon shown on the right on the Apps screen.

Settings

In addition to the main **Settings** app, you can access some frequently used settings using the **Quick Settings** screen shown below. Swipe down once (or twice, if necessary) from the top of the screen to display the **Quick Settings**.

Battery   Display main **Settings**

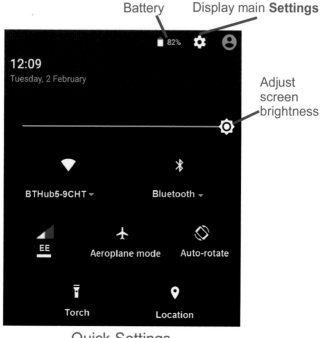

Adjust screen brightness

Quick Settings

The above features are discussed on the next page.

The icons on the **Quick Settings** screen on the previous page have the following functions:

 Displays % of battery charge remaining.

 Tap to display main **Settings** app.

 Adjust screen brightness by sliding the icon.

 Tap to display SIM card information for your cell phone network such as **EE** in this example.

Switches on the Quick Settings Screen
The following switches are shown in the **On** state on page 96. When **Off** they are greyed out with a line through them.

 Connection to a Wi-Fi network.

 Bluetooth wireless connection over short distances to other Bluetooth *paired* devices.

 Aeroplane or **Flight Mode**. Switches off the Internet so that the phone can be used on a flight.

 Auto-rotate. Rotate the screen display automatically when the phone is turned.

 Switch on the LED **Torch** on the back of the phone.

Switch on **Location** services to allow the phone to pinpoint your current location.

The Settings App

This allows you to set up or modify all of the settings on the Android phone.

- On most versions of Android, tap the **All Apps** icon on the **Favorites Tray**, on the Home Screen, as shown on the right and below.

  This opens the Apps screen as shown on page 106.

- On Android Nougat tap the small arrow or swipe up the Home Screen, shown in part below, to open the Apps screen.

- Tap the **Settings** icon shown on the right on the Apps screen to open the **Settings** app shown on the next page.

Although the colours and layout may change, the basic settings are the same on all versions of Android.

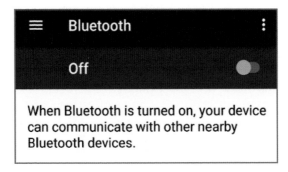

Tap on any of the headings listed above to view information, optional settings and **ON** or **OFF** switches, as shown in the **Bluetooth** example below.

Notifications

At the top left of the of the Home and Apps screens you can see a group of small icons, similar to those shown below.

The icons above represent notifications or messages to let you know an event has occurred such as:

- An e-mail has been received.
- A file has been uploaded or downloaded to or from the Internet.
- A screenshot has been captured.
- Some apps have been updated.
- A system update is available.

To display your notifications in full, swipe down from the top left of the screen. If a notification refers to an e-mail, tap twice to read the message. Once you've looked at a notification, it's removed from the list.

The Status Bar

This is a group of icons at the top right of the screen, such as those shown in the example below.

The icon on the extreme left above indicates that Wi-Fi is connected. **4G** and the triangle denote a connection to a cell phone network. The rectangular icon shows the state of charge of the battery. While a battery is being charged, a lightning strike appears on the battery icon, as shown on the right.

9

Screens and Apps

Introduction

This chapter describes the three main types of screen on Android smartphones and tablets. These are:

- The Lock Screen
- The Home Screen
- The Apps Screen

The Lock Screen

The *Lock Screen* can be used as a security device to prevent other people using your phone. It's the first screen you see when you power up the computer.

Alternative backgrounds or **Wallpapers** are discussed on page 122.

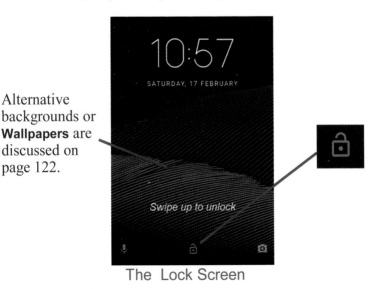

The Lock Screen

Displaying The Lock Screen

To start the phone, hold down the **Power Button**, shown on page 19, for a few seconds until the Lock Screen is displayed, as shown on the previous page. (There are options to change the background wallpaper, as discussed later in this chapter.) The Lock Screen also appears when the phone has been switched on but unused for some time and when you press the power button

The Lock Screen on later Androids also shows *notifications*, i.e. short messages informing you, for example, that you've received an e-mail or a file has been *downloaded* from the Internet and saved on your phone. Tap on the notification for more information.

Notifications

The Lock Screen

Opening the Home Screen

Place a finger near the bottom of Lock Screen and *swipe* or slide it upwards. This opens the *Home Screen*, shown on the next page. Other more secure options to unlock the Lock Screen and access the Home Screen, such as a PIN, pattern or fingerprint recognition are discussed on page 175.

The Home Screen

The Home Screen is opened as described at the bottom of page 102. Shown below is the Nougat Home Screen

The Home Screen

In fact there are several Home Screens on an Android smartphone or tablet. The central Home Screen shown above has a number of pre-installed apps and you can install more from the Play Store, as discussed in Chapter 10. You can move between the various Home screens by swiping left or right, as discussed on the next page.

- Swipe right across the screen to display the Google Search Bar and news items, including world news, local news and items reflecting topics you've previously searched for.

- Swiping left across the screen produces a similar screen to the central Home Screen shown on page 103. This can be used to add icons to give easy access to apps you use frequently.

- Swipe left or right to return to the central Home Screen.

- To return to the central Home Screen while running an app, tap the circle icon on the Navigation Bar at the bottom of the screen, shown below.

The Favorites Tray
Android Lollipop, Marshmallow, etc.

Along the bottom of all the Home Screens is the *Favorites Tray* shown below, giving quick access to frequently used apps.

As discussed shortly, you can swap most of the icons on the Favorites Tray to give quick access to frequently used apps.

As shown above and on the right, there is a row of dots just above the Favorites Tray, indicating which Home screen is currently displayed. The example on the right shows that the central Home screen is selected.

The All Apps Icon

The *All Apps* icon shown on the right and on the Favorites Tray above is a permanent fixture in the centre of the Favorites Tray. Tapping this icon opens the *Apps Screen*, as shown on the next page. This displays all the apps installed on the smartphone or tablet.

All Apps

Android Nougat

This version of Android does not show the three dots to indicate which Home screen is currently being displayed.

Also, as discussed on page 98, instead of tapping the All Apps icon shown above, the Nougat Apps screen is opened by tapping the icon shown on the right or by swiping up the screen.

105

The Apps Screen

This contains a number of apps pre-installed on a new smartphone or tablet. In addition you can install further apps from the Google Play Store, as discussed in Chapter 10. The Apps Screen used on Android Nougat is shown below. Earlier versions of Android may use a different background colour but are otherwise very similar.

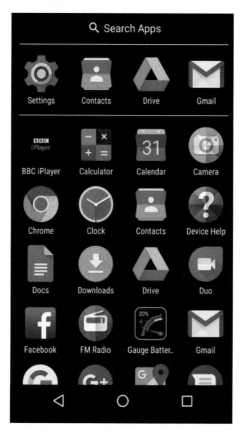

As discussed on page 120, your favourite icons can be copied from the Apps Screens to blank spaces on your Home Screen to make a personal Home Screen.

Also, as you continue to use apps, icons for the four apps you use most frequently are placed in the bar at the top of the Apps Screen, as shown below on Android Nougat.

The icons shown above are replaced automatically if you start to use other apps more frequently.

Navigating the Screens

Earlier Versions of Android

The Navigation Bar shown below is used to switch between the different screens, in addition to the methods of swiping left or right or tapping the All Apps icon shown on page 105. The Navigation Bar appears along the bottom of all the Home screens.

Navigation Bar: Early Versions of Android

- The left-hand button above opens the previous screen.

- The button in the middle opens the central Home Screen.

- The right-hand button on the Navigation Bar shown above displays *thumbnails* or small images of previously visited apps as shown on the next page.

- The right-hand button on the Navigation Bar is shown on the right and on the previous page. This displays thumbnails of the recently visited apps, as shown below, on Android Jelly Bean and KitKat versions.

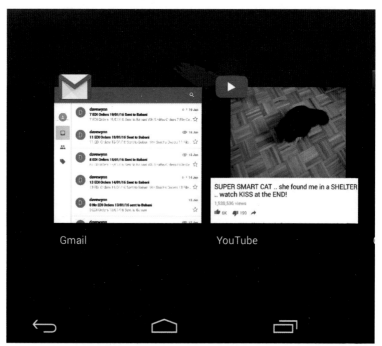

Recently Used Apps: Earlier Versions of Android

- The thumbnails can be scrolled horizontally across the screen.

- Tap a thumbnail for a previously visited app such as **Gmail** or **YouTube** shown above to open the App on the full screen.

Navigating the Screens

Later Versions of Android including Nougat

Lollipop, Marshmallow and Nougat use a slightly different Navigation Bar, as shown below.

Navigation Bar: Later Versions of Android

- The left-hand button opens the previous screen.
- The middle button opens the central Home Screen.
- The right-hand button opens a revolving carousel of "cards" representing the recently visited apps, also known as *Overview Mode*, as shown below.

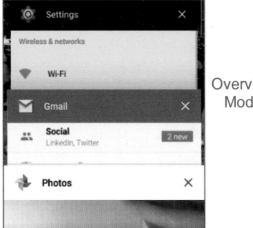

Overview
Mode

Recent Apps: Later Versions of Android

- Swipe up or down to scroll through all of the cards.
- Tap anywhere on a card open the app on the screen.
- Tap the cross on a card to close the app.

Icons for Popular Android Apps

 All Apps: displays all the apps installed on a device.

 Google Chrome: a popular Web browser for navigating the Internet.

 Google Play Store: the source for downloading apps.

 Google: *search engine* used to find information on any subject after *typing* or *speaking* the *keywords*.

 Google Earth: photos and satellite images of places around the world, including Google Street View.

 Google Mail or **Gmail**: an electronic mail service.

 Play Music: install and play music, create playlists.

 Play Movies & TV: rent or buy then download.

 Google Maps: Searchable maps of the world with facilities to zoom in and zoom out.

Google+: a social network allowing you to share updates and photos, etc.

 Google Drive: cloud storage area which also includes free word processing and spreadsheet software.

 Dropbox: cloud storage area allowing photos and files, etc., to be accessed from any computer.

 Play Books: Download and read eBooks from the Google Play Store and create your own library.

 Kindle: Download and read eBooks from the Amazon Kindle Store.

 Skype: Internet telephone service allowing free video calls between computers around the world.

 Facebook: the popular social networking Web site.

 Twitter: social networking using "tweets" or short messages.

 Hangouts: send messages to your friends or start a video call.

 Camera: Use front facing camera for video calls and "selfies" or rear camera for general photography.

WhatsApp: free worldwide phone calls using a smartphone and the Internet.

 Photos: view, edit, share and manage your photographs.

 BBC iPlayer: watch live, catchup and television on demand.

 ITV Hub: watch live, catchup and television on demand.

 YouTube: watch free videos, e.g. amusing incidents, uploaded to the Internet for other people to share.

Versions of Android

The icons above on this page and on pages 110 and 111 are reproduced from Nougat (Android 7.0), currently the latest widely available version of Android. Earlier versions of Android use slightly different icons as shown below. (Earlier versions of Android are shown on the left, Nougat on the right).

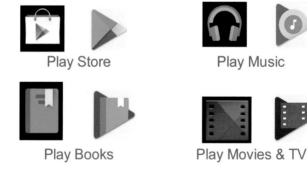

Play Store   Play Music

Play Books   Play Movies & TV

Managing Apps and Widgets

Introduction

When you buy a new Android smartphone or tablet, many apps are already installed, as shown on the Apps Screen on page 106. In December 2017 3.5 million apps were available to be downloaded from the Google Play Store, many of them free. Some apps are initially free, but may later offer *in-app purchases* for additional features or more professional versions of the software.

This chapter covers the following:

- Searching for apps from the many categories available in the Play Store.

- Downloading apps from the Play Store and installing them on your phone or tablet.

- Customising Your Favorites Tray and Home Screen, etc.

- Copying apps to make a personal Home Screen for your frequently used apps.

- Organising apps into *folders* for different categories.

- Working with *widgets* — similar to apps but displaying information such as a calendar.

The Google Play Store

To launch the **Play Store**, tap its icon (shown on the right) on the Home Screen or on the Apps Screen. The **Google Play** window opens, displaying the **HOME** screen shown below.

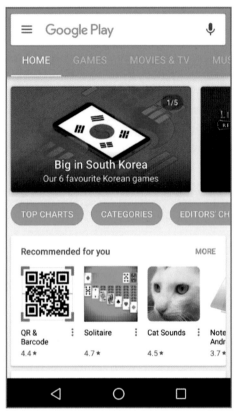

The Google Play Store

Scroll left from **HOME**, **GAMES**, **MOVIES & TV**, shown above to view **MUSIC**, **BOOKS** and **NEWSSTAND**. Tap any of these to view the available apps or media such as movies or eBooks.

Although known as the Play Store, it actually contains apps in many categories other than games, such as business, music and utilities to help with the running of your smartphone or tablet.

Tapping **CATEGORIES** shown on the previous page displays apps on a wide range of subjects, as shown in the small extract below.

Categories of App in the Play Store

To view all of the **Top categories** above swipe or scroll the top row of icons left or scroll upwards to view **All categories**.

Browsing the Play Store for Apps

Select a **CATEGORY** such as **Health & Fitness**, shown below, then browse through to find an app you're interested in.

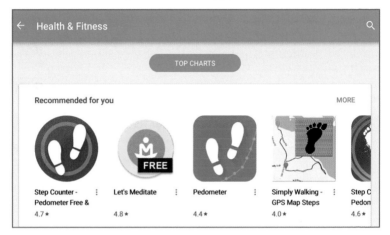

Health and Fitness Apps

Tap on the image of the app to read a description.

Many of the apps in the Play Store are free. Tap on a free app to display the **INSTALL** button shown on the right and then tap to download the app to your smartphone or tablet.

If the app is not free, the price is displayed at the bottom of the listing for the app, as shown below. Tap the price to choose your payment method before completing the purchase and installing the app.

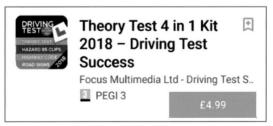

Searching the Play Store for Apps

Tap the icon shown on the right to open the Play Store.

Typing the Keywords

The search bar appears as shown below, ready for you to type the name of the app you wish to search for.

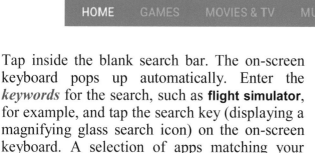

Tap inside the blank search bar. The on-screen keyboard pops up automatically. Enter the *keywords* for the search, such as **flight simulator**, for example, and tap the search key (displaying a magnifying glass search icon) on the on-screen keyboard. A selection of apps matching your search keywords is displayed as shown below.

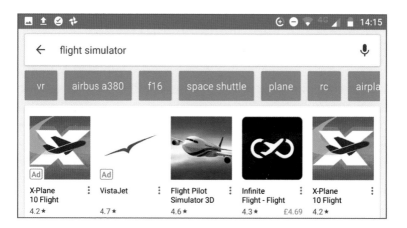

Searching Using Speech Recognition

Tap the microphone icon shown on the right and below.

The small window shown below appears, requiring you to speak the keywords, such as **flight simulator**, for example.

You might like to practise searching for a few apps using the microphone, such as **chess**, **route planner** and **sound recorder**, for example.

Downloading and Installing an App

Tap the app you wish to install and if the app is not free, tap the price and buy the app online. Now tap **INSTALL** and wait a few minutes for the app to be downloaded to your Apps screen and your Home Screen, shown below. Tap the icon to start using the newly installed app such as **Flight Pilot** in this example, as shown below.

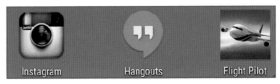

In-app Purchases

When you tap an app in the Play Store, you may see the words **In-app purchases** under the **INSTALL** button as shown on the right. This

In-app purchases

means that although the app itself is free, you may be asked to make extra payments associated with the app. These payments might be for additional features or to purchase a "professional" version of the app rather than the basic or free edition. Some games allow you to buy additional features or even pay to advance to a higher level.

It may be possible for someone else, especially children, to use your smartphone or tablet to run up a huge bill by making **In-app purchases**. The solution is to set a password which is required for all purchases from the Play Store.

Tap the Play Store menu icon shown on the left and below.

Then scroll down the menu and select **Settings**. From the **Settings** menu switch **Parental controls ON** and tap **Apps and Games**. Then type a suitable **PIN** number as shown below and tap **OK**.

Customising the Favorites Tray
Android Marshmallow, Lollipop, KitKat, etc.

The Favorites Tray on the Home Screens is shown below. The All Apps icon shown on the right and below is a fixture on the Favorites Tray — it cannot be moved or deleted. The other icons can be moved and replaced with any other apps you prefer.

Removing an App from the Favorites Tray

Touch and hold the app you want to remove from the Favorites Tray until **X Remove** appears at the top of the screen. Drag the icon over **X Remove** and drop it, deleting the app. Removing an app from the Favorites Tray doesn't uninstall the app from the Apps Screen. Alternatively, move an app from the Favorites Tray and slide it onto another part of the Home Screen.

Moving an App to the Favorites Tray

Clear a space on the Favorites Tray by moving or removing an icon, as described above. To move an app on the Home Screen to the Favorites Tray, tap and hold the icon, then drag the icon to the newly cleared space on the Favorites Tray. In the example below, the icon for the **Camera** app shown on the right of the Favorites Tray above has been removed and replaced by an icon for a *folder* which includes the various **Google** apps.

Android Nougat

As discussed on page 105, the All Apps icon does not appear on Nougat. Instead you have to tap the small arrow shown below or swipe up the screen to open the Apps Screen, also known as the *Apps Drawer*.

The Favorites Tray on Nougat has only 5 icons and these can be removed or replaced like those on earlier versions of Android on page 120. The small arrow shown above is a permanent fixture, replacing the All Apps icon shown at the top right of page 120.

Customising Your Home Screen

When you start using a new smartphone or tablet, you can tailor the Home Screen to suit your own requirements, as follows:

- Change the background colour or wallpaper.
- Copy apps from the Apps Screen and place them on on the Home Screen for easy access.
- Delete any apps and widgets you no longer need.

You can group apps into *folders*, which can be added to the Home Screen and to the Favourites Tray. Folders are discussed on page 124.

Changing the Wallpaper on Your Home Screen

Hold your finger on an empty part of the Home Screen until the **WALLPAPERS** icon shown below appears.

Tap **WALLPAPERS** shown above and then select your chosen pattern or design. The wallpaper can also be a photo of your own. Then tap **SET WALLPAPER** at the top right of the screen.

WIDGETS shown above are similar to apps but are used to display news and information, as discussed on page 125.

SETTINGS shown above allows you to set **Home Screen rotation ON** or **OFF**. When screen rotation is **ON** and the phone or tablet is turned from portrait to landscape, say, the screen display rotates so that it's still easy to read.

Adding Apps to Your Home Screen

To make up a personal Home Screen displaying only the apps you find most useful, open the Home Screen where you want the apps to appear. Clear the screen of any apps and widgets you don't want. This is done by touching and holding the app or widget, then dragging it onto **X Remove**, as described previously.

Next open the Apps Screen containing the app you want to copy. On Android Nougat, swipe up the screen or tap the arrow shown on the right to open the Apps Screen.

On Marshmallow, Lollipop, KitKat, etc., tap the All Apps icon as shown on the right to open the Apps Screen.

Tap and hold the app you want to copy to the Home Screen. The Home Screen opens. Keeping your finger on the app, slide it into the required position on the Home Screen. Part of a personal Home Screen is shown below. The top two rows of apps have been copied from the Apps screen.

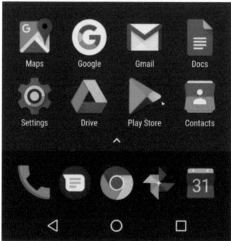

A Personal Home Screen

Deleting Apps from the Home Screen

Tap and hold an unwanted app until **X Remove** appears at the top of the screen. Then drag the app over **X Remove** to delete it. Apps deleted from the Home Screen are only *copies* — the apps still exist on the Apps Screen.

Unlike apps removed from the Home Screen, apps *uninstalled* from the Apps Screen are completely removed from the tablet. If the uninstalled apps are needed in the future, they will need to be reinstalled from the *Play Store*.

Organising Apps in Folders
Marshmallow, Lollipop, KitKat, etc.

Folders containing several apps, as shown on the right, can be created on the Home Screen and on the Favorites Tray. For example, you could put the apps for **Facebook**, **Twitter**, **Skype** and **Google+**, shown below on the Home Screen, in a folder called **Social**.

Touch and drag the icons, one on top of the other, to form a single circular folder icon shown on the left below. Tap the folder icon to reveal the contents and to name the folder. As shown below, tap **Unnamed Folder** and enter a name of your choice, **Social** in this example. Tap a folder icon to view and launch the individual apps within, as shown in the middle below.

The above methods are the same for Nougat phones and tablets, except for the folder icon which appears as shown on the right.

Widgets

A *widget* is an icon used to display information such as a calendar, your most recent e-mails, or a digital clock, including the weather, as shown on the right. Widgets can appear alongside of the apps you have installed on the Home Screen, as shown below.

Digital clock, calendar and weather widget

A Widget on the Home Screen

Tapping a widget displays more information, on the full screen. In the example above, tapping the icons shown on the right displays a detailed weather forecast. Tapping on the time displays a full screen, digital clock with options to set an **ALARM**, use as a **TIMER** or use as a **STOPWATCH**. Tapping the date on the widget shown above displays a full screen calendar.

Viewing the Installed Widgets

Tap and hold an empty part of the Home Screen until the **WIDGETS** icon appears as shown right and on page122. Tap the **WIDGETS** icon to see those widgets already installed on your phone or tablet, such as the **Calendar** widget shown below.

Tap and hold a widget in the **WIDGETS** screen to add it to your Home Screen. You can find many more widgets in the the Play Store, after entering **widgets** in the search bar in the Play Store or on the Apps screen. Examples of widgets are:

- Local weather forecasts
- Your e-mail inbox
- An analogue or digital clock
- Newspaper headlines and articles
- A calendar
- A battery charge indicator

Widgets are installed, copied to the Home Screen and deleted in the same way as apps, as described earlier.

Browsing the Web

Introduction

The Android smartphone gives us access to millions of Web pages, containing the latest information on any subject you can think of.

The Chrome Web browser is a Google product, like the Android operating system itself. Chrome enables you to search millions of Web pages quickly and easily and displays the results in an attractive and readable format. The Google search engine is the world's leading Web search program on all platforms – smartphone, tablet, laptop etc. So the Android phone is an ideal tool for browsing the Internet to find information. This activity alone justifies the purchase of an Android phone, not to mention its many other functions such as phone calls, text messages, social networking and entertainment, discussed shortly.

Some of the main functions of Google Chrome are:

- To search for and display information after entering or speaking *keywords* into the search bar.

- To access Web pages after entering an *address*, such as **www.babanibooks.com**, into the browser.

- To move between Web pages by tapping *links* or *hyperlinks* on a Web page and move forwards and backwards between Web pages.

- To use *tabs* to switch between open Web pages.

- To *bookmark* Web pages for revisiting at a later time.

Launching Google Chrome

To launch Google Chrome, tap its icon on the Apps Screen or on the Favorites Tray, shown below.

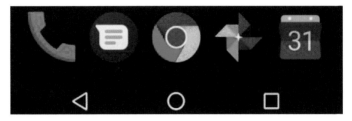

The search bar across the top of the screen, shown below, is the place to start your Web browsing activities. Here you enter either the *address* of a Web site or *keywords* which should pinpoint the subject you are interested in.

Search or type web address	🎤

Searching for a Web Site Address

Every Web site has a unique address, known as its *URL*, or *Uniform Resource Locator*. A typical Web address is :

www.babanibooks.com

- Type the URL into the search bar, as shown below. As you start typing, the microphone icon shown above disappears and is replaced by the cross below.

www.babanibooks.com	✖

- Tap the **Go** or arrow key (shown on the right) on the on-screen keyboard to start the search.

Using the Microphone

Instead of typing the URL, you can tap the microphone icon shown on the right and on the previous page. Then speak the Web address.

The Search Result

After entering the address of the Web site into the search bar and pressing **Go** or the arrow key on the on-screen keyboard, the Web site's Home Page should quickly open on the screen, as shown in the extract below.

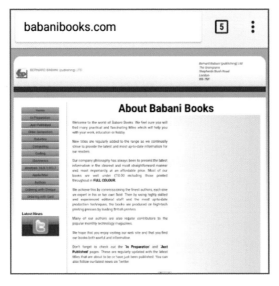

The Keyword Search

This is used to find out about a particular *subject* rather than visiting a Web site whose address you already know, as discussed on the previous page. For example, suppose you want to find out about the **Great Wall of China**. Enter the keywords as shown on the next page or tap the microphone icon and speak them.

Predictive Text

As you start entering the keywords, Google makes suggestions underneath, as shown below. If correct, tap this *predictive text* to save you typing all of the keywords which make up the search criteria.

After completing the entry of the keywords and tapping the **Go** or arrow key on the on-screen keyboard, a list of Google search results is displayed, as shown in the sample below.

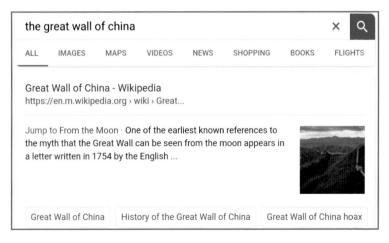

As shown on the previous page, there's no need to use capital letters when typing the search criteria — **the great wall of china** yields the same results as **The Great Wall Of China**.

A search may yield thousands of results and these can be viewed by swiping upwards. Google places the most significant results near the top of the list. However, some results may be irrelevant to a particular search. For example, anyone studying the **Great Wall of China** may not be particularly interested in the **Great Wall Chinese Restaurant** which appears in the results of the search.

The blue heading on a search result, shown below, represents a *link* to a Web page which contains the keywords you've entered.

Great Wall of China: Great Wall Tours, Facts, History, Photos
www.travelchinaguide.com › china_great...

Tap a link to have a look at the Web site as shown below.

As shown on the previous page, you can also see the results of your search organised in various categories such as **IMAGES**, **MAPS**, **VIDEOS** and **NEWS**, etc.

Searching for Anything

The Web is surely the world's largest and most up-to-date encyclopaedia covering almost every known subject, no matter how bizarre. For example, type any task, such as **grooming a dog that bites** and numerous Web sites offer helpful advice, including step-by-step videos.

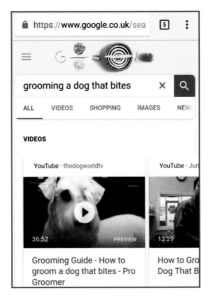

Try typing a few diverse keywords into Google Chrome and see how easy it is to find good information on virtually any subject. Here's a few random examples to get you started:

mending a puncture	sopwith camel	tesla
brunel	ann of cleves	growing orchids
ssd	usb	halebop
samuel johnson	boadicea	cpu

Surfing the Net

After opening a Web page from the results of a search, as shown below, words highlighted in blue are *hyperlinks*, also known simply as *links*.

Tap a blue text link shown above to open further relevant Web pages. Each new page will usually have further links to open a succession of Web pages.

Previously Visited Pages

As you follow links on a Web site, you may wish to return to a previous Web page. This can be done using the arrow button on the Navigation Bar at the bottom of the screen.

Using Tabs

Tabs allow you to switch easily between all of the Web sites currently open on your phone. This section describes tabs as used on phones using Android Nougat and Marshmallow.

Tabs are displayed in *Overview Mode*, as shown below. Overview Mode is also used to display currently open apps as discussed on page 109.

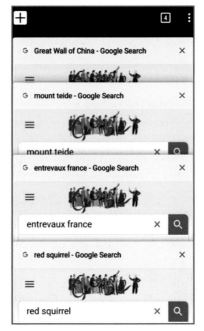

Tabs in Overview Mode: Android Phone

Swipe up, if necessary, to scroll through all of the Web sites then tap on the one you wish to open fully on the screen.

Android *tablets* also use tabs for moving between Web sites but with the tabs displayed horizontally across the screen rather than as cards in Overview Mode as shown above.

Opening a New Tab

When you launch Chrome by tapping its icon on the Home Screen or Apps Screen, the following screen appears.

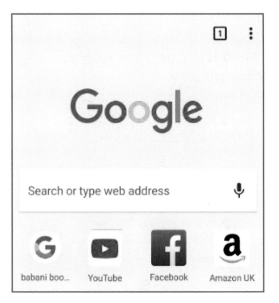

If you are just starting to use Chrome, the icons above such as **YouTube** and **Facebook** represent popular Web sites. If you are an experienced user of Chrome, sites you have used regularly are also listed.

To open a new tab, tap the 3-dot menu button shown on the right and in the screenshot above. The following menu opens, including the option to open a **New tab.**

New tab

New incognito tab

Close all tabs

Now enter search criteria such as **red squirrel** in the search bar as shown below and tap the search icon.

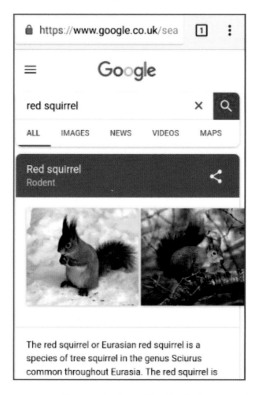

Now to open another tab, tap the 3-dot menu button again and again select **New tab** from the menu which appears, as shown in the extract below.

This open the new search screen again, as shown on page 135, in which to enter some new search criteria. Entering **buzzard**, for example, opens the Web page shown below.

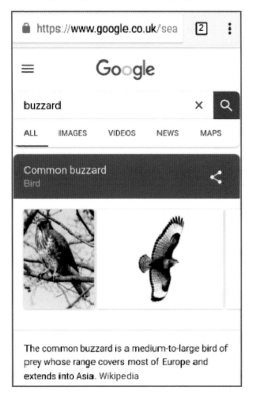

As you continue creating new tabs, the number of tabs currently open is displayed in a box to the top right of the address bar at the top of the screen, also shown on the right and below.

- To display all of the tabs in Overview Mode, as shown below, tap on the numbered square shown on the right and on the previous page. The + icon on the top left below can be tapped to quickly start a new tab.

red squirrel - Google Search

Google

buzzard - Google Search

Google

buzzard

ALL   IMAGES   VIDEOS   NEWS   MAPS

barn owl - Google Search

Google

barn owl

ALL   IMAGES   VIDEOS   SHOPPING   NEW

- To open one of the Web sites fully on the screen, as shown on the previous two pages, tap anywhere on the tab.

- To close a tab, tap the cross in the top right-hand corner of the tab, as shown above.

Starting a New Session

If you switch the phone off while several tabs containing Web pages are still open, next time you switch on and select Chrome, the tabs will still be present.

- Tap the numbered square shown below to open the tabs in Overview Mode as shown on page 138.

- Then tap on a tab to display a Web page fully.

Closing All Tabs

- Display the tabs in Overview Mode, as shown on page 138.
- Tap the 3-dot menu button, shown on the right and above, to open the menu shown below.

New tab

New incognito tab

Close all tabs

- Select **Close all tabs** from the above menu.

Private Browsing

Chrome normally remembers your browsing activities. So someone with access to your computer could find out what you've been doing. This can be prevented by selecting **New incognito tab** from the menu shown above to make your browsing activities private using that particular tab.

Split-screen Mode (Nougat Onwards)

This feature allows you to open two apps simultaneously on the screen. Shown below in the top half of the screen is the Google Chrome app displaying tabs for Venice, Florence and Milan. In this mode the tabs are displayed and scrolled horizontally, not like the vertical tabs or cards in Overview Mode shown on page 138. In this example, the Calendar app is open in the bottom half of the screen.

Chrome app
showing tabs for
open Web pages

Chrome
Split-screen
Mode

Calendar app

- To switch Split-screen mode **On**, open the first app and touch and hold down the square Overview Mode button shown on the right and on the Navigation Bar below.

- The square icon on the Navigation Bar changes to the Split-screen icon shown on the right.

- Tap to open an app listed in the lower half of the screen or launch a new app from the apps screen.

- To close Split-screen mode, hold down the icon shown again on the right.

Viewing Previously Visited Web Pages

With a Web page open as shown on pages 138 and 140, tap the 3-dot menu button to open the menu shown below.

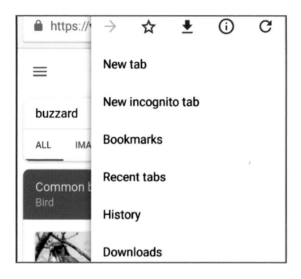

Bookmarks

- Tap the star icon shown on the right and above to *Bookmark* the current Web page for future retrieval and viewing. ☆

- Tap **Bookmarks** on the above menu to select previously bookmarked Web pages you wish to open.

Your Browsing History

The **History** option shown on the previous page automatically lists the Web pages you've visited in recent weeks, in chronological order, with the latest at the top. However, any Web pages you opened in *incognito tabs*, i.e. *private browsing*, as discussed on page 139, will not appear in the **History** list.

History   Q   ✕

CLEAR BROWSING DATA...

G   san marino - Google Search   🗑
      www.google.co.uk

G   milan - Google Search   🗑
      www.google.co.uk

G   rome - Google Search   🗑
      www.google.co.uk

- Tap a Web page in the list to open it on the screen.

Clearing Your Browsing History

- Tap **CLEAR BROWSING DATA...** at the top of the **History** list shown above to remove all of the Web pages opened over a selected time period i.e. the **Last hour**, **24 hours**, **7days**, **4 weeks** or **All time**.
- Then tap **CLEAR DATA**.

Downloading a Web Page

- To save a Web page on your phone for reading later *offline*, i.e. where there is no Internet, tap the *Download* icon shown on the right. The page can be reopened later offline, after selecting **Downloads** shown on page 141.

Entertainment

Introduction

The following activities are discussed in this chapter:

- eBooks — electronic books which may be read *online* or downloaded from the Internet for reading *offline* at any time.

- Music, movies and games downloaded for free or bought or rented.

- YouTube — a Google-owned Web site enabling you to play free music and videos uploaded by other people.

- Live and catchup TV and radio.

The small size and light weight of an Android smartphone mean you can use it literally anywhere — on a train, in bed or in a public place such as a restaurant. You can stow it in a bag and take it on holiday; most hotels have free Wi-Fi so while you're away you can still go online for all your favourite Internet activities. The Android device may also be used for your personal in-flight entertainment, if the airline allows it. *Aeroplane mode* or *flight mode* should be switched on in **Settings** to prevent possible interference with the aircraft's instruments. This only allows you to use the smartphone or tablet *offline*, i.e. not connected to the Internet. Offline activities would include reading an e-Book which has been downloaded and saved on the Internal Storage of the phone or tablet, before boarding the aircraft.

Browsing Through the Play Store Books

Open the Play Store, as shown below, by tapping its icon shown on the right. Then scroll across from **HOME**, **GAMES**, etc., to **BOOKS**, shown below.

You can browse through the books under various headings such as **TOP SELLING** and **NEW RELEASES**, **GENRES** and **COMICS** partly shown below.

Tap **GENRES** shown above to see the categories of books available. Select a genre, such as **Cookery**, **Food and Wine**, to see the range of those particular books available in the Play Store, as shown in the small sample below.

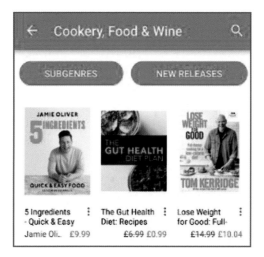

Using Google Play Books

When you first start to use an Android smartphone, there is already an icon for the Play Books app on the Apps screen. If you read a lot of eBooks, for easy access you may wish to copy the icon to the Favorites Tray, if it's not already there, as discussed on page 120.

Earlier Android   Nougat

Tap the Play Books icon shown above. The Google Play Books app opens as shown below with the **Home** screen displayed.

As shown above there are **EBOOKS** and **AUDIOBOOKS**. Scroll up the screen to see books recommended for you and top selling books in each category.

Selecting **Library** as shown on the previous page displays books you've already added. On a brand new Android phone, you'll probably find some books are already installed.

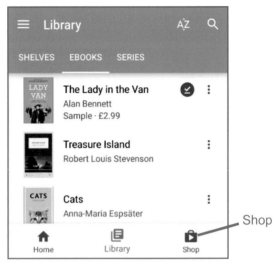

Shop

Downloading

Books displaying the tick icon shown on the right have been downloaded and saved on your phone for reading *offline*. Books without a tick are in your library but can only be read when you are *online*.

Tap the 3-dot button shown on the right of each of the books listed above. This opens the menu shown below, including the option to **Download** a copy.

Buy

Download

Delete from library

Shopping for Books

Select **Shop** shown on the previous page and tap the search icon shown on the right. Then enter the subject or the title of a book you are interested in. Or tap the microphone icon shown on the right below and speak the keywords for the book search.

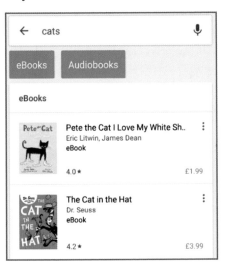

Tap a book cover for more details, to read a **FREE SAMPLE,** read reviews or to buy the book. Or tap the 3-dot button to the right of the book listing to open the menu shown below.

Buying a book requires a Google account and your bank account details.

Reading an eBook

Play Books

- Tap the **Play Books** icon on the Apps screen, then select **Library** shown below.

- Then tap the cover of the book you want to read. The book opens on the screen.

- Scroll backwards and forwards through the pages by swiping to the left or right, or tapping in the left and right margins.

- Tap anywhere on the text of the current page to view information about the page and to display various icons, etc., as shown in the top and bottom margins of the sample page below.

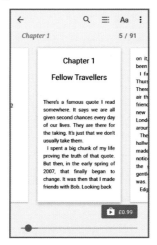

- Tap anywhere over the text again to switch off the icons and information.

- Drag the blue ball slider shown below to advance rapidly forward or backward through the book.

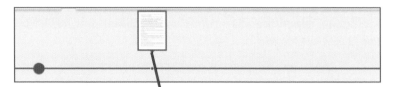

- Tap the page thumbnail shown above to return to the page you were previously reading.

- Across the top of the page, as shown above and on the previous page, chapter number and page number are displayed when you tap over a page. The icons on the top right above have the following functions:

 Search for certain words and highlight them where they occur in the text.

 List chapter headings, page numbers and bookmarks.

 Change the brightness and formatting such as size of text, line spacing and font, etc.

Open a menu, including options to add a bookmark or **Read aloud** as a *talking book*.

Bookmarks

- Tap in the right-hand corner of the screen and select **Add bookmark**, as shown on the right. Tap a bookmark to remove it.

Music in the Play Store

The methods used for obtaining and listening to music are very similar to those described earlier for books. Open the Play Store as described and tap **MUSIC** as shown below.

Then browse for the music you want, using the various **Genres**, such as **Classical**, **Folk** or **Pop** and **Top Albums**, **New Releases** or **Top Songs**, etc.

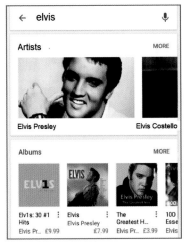

Alternatively tap the magnifying glass search icon, shown on the right, then enter the name of a piece of music or an artist.

Tap the Play Music icon shown on the right and select the music you want to play.

Google Play Movies & TV

The Play Store contains a range of movies and TV shows in various categories, etc., as shown below.

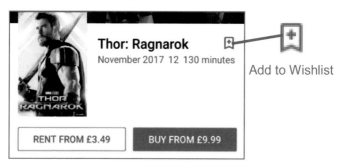

A movie may be bought or rented. You may have to begin watching a movie within 30 days of renting it and the rental may expire 48 hours after you start watching it.

Add to Wishlist

Tap **RENT** or **BUY** and after completing the transaction, watch the movie after tapping the **Play Movies & TV** icon shown on the right and selecting **Library**.

Downloading a Movie for Viewing Offline

Moon

To make a movie watchable offline, tap the **Download** icon shown on the right and on the movie graphic on the left. The circle starts to fill with red "ink" and when completely full the download is complete. The arrrow icon changes to a white tick in a red circle, as shown on the right.

YouTube

YouTube is a Web site, owned by Google, which provides a platform for people to share videos which they've recorded themselves. These can rapidly become very popular and "go viral", watched by millions of people around the world.

To launch YouTube, tap the icon shown on the right, on the Apps screen. The YouTube screen shows a long list of video clips which can be scrolled up and down by swiping through various categories.

Live and Catchup Television and Radio

The Google Play Store includes the free BBC iPlayer app. This can be installed on your phone or tablet as described in Chapter 10. Tap the icon shown on the right to open the BBC iPlayer as shown below.

BBC iPlayer

Tap **Menu** shown above left to choose from programmes on different channels including radio and in various **Categories** such as **Comedy**, **Documentaries**, **Drama & Soaps** and **Entertainment**.

Watching TV

Tap anywhere on the picture for the episode, programme, etc., and then tap the play button. The screen display has the normal play, pause and volume control buttons.

Games

There are thousands of games in the Google Play Store, many of them free, though some include *In-app purchases* to buy extras, as discussed on page 119. Games are downloaded and installed as discussed in Chapter 10 and so they will be available to play offline. Games, like apps, can be removed from your phone as discussed on page 123.

Ultimate Cat ⋮
Simulator
4.4★   £0.89

If you play a lot of games, you may wish to organize them into *folders*, as discussed on page 124. In this example, the four games on the right have been grouped into a single folder, as shown below.

My Games folder

Communication and Social Networking

Introduction

This chapter describes briefly some of the many apps used to communicate with other people, in addition to normal calls over a cell phone network These include:

Gmail

Google e-mail used by businesses, friends and families to send messages and photos all over the world.

Skype

Free worldwide *voice* and *video* calls.

Facebook

Enter your personal *profile* and *timeline* and make *online friends* with people having similar interests.

Twitter

Another very popular social networking site, based on short text messages (280 characters maximum).

WhatsApp

A free service for sending text messages, photos and documents using smartphones.

Instagram

This makes it easy to take photos and videos and share them with other people.

Snapchat

Take photos and send them with *Stories* to friends in instant messages, available for a limited time only.

Electronic Mail

Gmail is used for creating, sending and receiving text messages over the Internet. *Replies* can easily be sent to the original sender of a message you've received and to all other recipients of the message or *forwarded* to someone else.

Gmail

You can maintain an *address book* for all your contacts and *import* into it files of contacts from other e-mail services.

An e-mail message can include photos and documents, known as *attachments*, "clipped" to the message.

Gmail is a Web-based e-mail service, so you can access your messages from anywhere in the world with access to the Internet, using your Gmail username and password.

The Gmail icon shown above gives access to Gmail and any other e-mail services you use. After tapping the Gmail icon, tap the 3-bar menu button and select the e-mail account you wish to use, as shown on the right.

Creating a Message

Tap the 3-bar menu button at the top left of the screen, shown above, then tap the **Compose** icon at the bottom right of the screen, shown here on the right. The **Compose** screen opens, as shown on the next page. Enter the main recipient's e-mail address in the **To** bar. Tapping the small arrow on the far right of **To** opens two new lines for recipients who will receive either Carbon copies (**Cc**) or Blind carbon copies (**Bcc**). The latter don't know who else has received a copy of the message.

Attach file Send

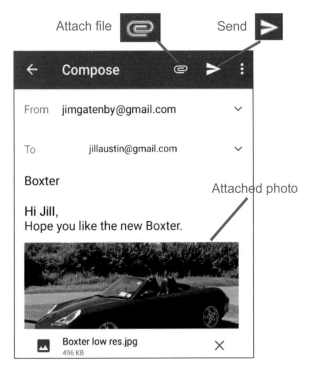

Attached photo

Receiving an E-mail

The recipient can read the e-mail in their *Inbox*. They will see the sender's name and the text and photos as shown above.

To open an attached document, tap its name or the paperclip icon, as shown on the right. Tap the star icon on the right to mark the e-mail as a *favourite*. Icons at the top and bottom of the **Inbox**, shown below, allow you to reply to the sender, reply to all recipients of the message or forward the e-mail to someone else.

Reply   Reply all   Forward

Skype

This app allows you to make *voice* and *video* calls all over the world. Calls over the Internet are free. You can also send photographs and instant text messages or make and send a video.

The Skype app in the Google Play Store is free and, if necessary, can be installed as described in Chapter 10.

Start Skype by tapping its icon on the All Apps screen, as shown on the right. Then sign in using an existing Skype username and password or a Microsoft account, or create a new Skype account. When you sign in, contacts from your address book are displayed, as shown below.

Skype

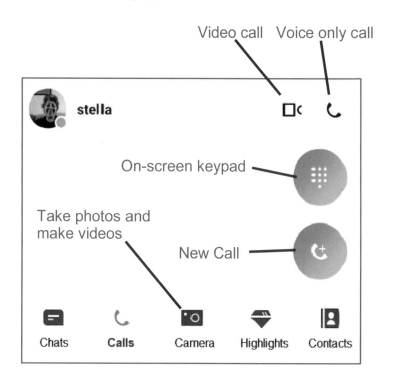

Making a Skype Call

As shown on the right, any contacts currently online are displayed with a green dot, as shown on the right and on the previous page.

stella

Tap the name or thumbnail of a contact who is currently online.

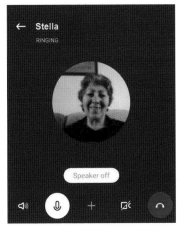

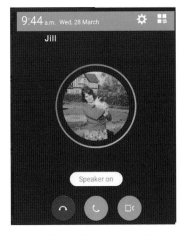

Making a Skype call

Receiving a call

As shown above and on the previous page, you can choose to make a voice only call or a video call. The video call allows you and your contact to see live images of each other and your respective surroundings. The voice only call shows the caller's profile photo on your screen.

The icon shown on the right and on the previous page presents an on-screen keypad, allowing you to dial a phone number, rather than a Skype contact. Calls over the Internet between smartphones, tablets and computers are free, but calls dialled to a landline or mobile phone number are charged to your Skype account.

Facebook

Facebook is the biggest social network, with over a billion users. To join Facebook, you must be aged over 13 years and have a valid e-mail address. You can access Facebook using the Android Facebook app, if necessary installed from the Play Store, as discussed in Chapter 10. You also need to *sign up* for a Facebook account and in future *sign in* with your e-mail address and password.

Facebook

First you create your own *Profile* in the form of a *Timeline*, as shown below. This can include biographical details such as your schools, employers and hobbies and interests. Facebook then provides lists of people with similar interests, who you may want to invite to be Facebook *friends*. Anyone who accepts will be able to exchange news, information, photos and videos with you.

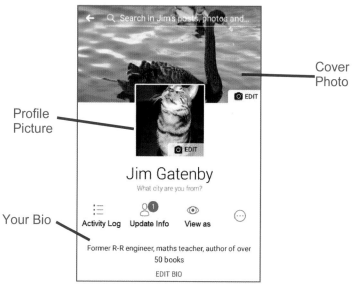

A Profile Picture or Cover Photo can be changed after tapping anywhere within the image.

Facebook Security and Privacy

The *audience selector* shown on the right appears against the items of personal information in your profile. Tapping the audience selector displays a drop-down menu, as shown on the right, enabling you to set the level of privacy for each item, ranging from **Public** to **Only me**. **Public** means *everyone* can see the information, including people you don't know.

Audience Selector

Status Updates

These are used to post your latest information and news and usually consist of a short text message and perhaps one or more photos, videos, etc., as shown below. Tap as shown below to select the audience. Then enter the text of your post, replacing **What's on your mind?** shown below. Finally tap SHARE to post your update.to friends, etc.

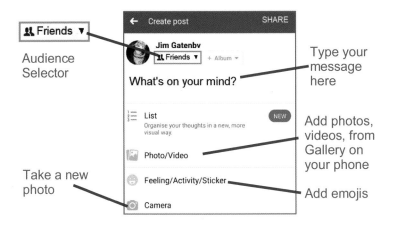

Audience Selector

Type your message here

Add photos, videos, from Gallery on your phone

Take a new photo

Add emojis

Twitter

Like Facebook, Twitter is a social networking website used by hundreds of millions of people. There is a free app for Twitter in the Google Play Store. If necessary, the app can be installed as discussed in Chapter 10. Signing up to Twitter is Twitter free. Once signed up you can either use your e-mail address and password to sign in or you can enter your Twitter username such as **@jimsmith**. Some of the main features of Twitter are:

- Twitter is a website used for posting text messages, known as *tweets*, of up to 280 characters in length.

- You can include a 160 character *personal profile* on your Twitter page.

- Photographs can be posted with a tweet.

- Twitter is based on people *following*, i.e. reading the tweets of friends, celebrities, companies, etc.

- You can follow anyone you like, but you can't choose who follows you. If you have no followers, anything you "tweet" will remain unread.

- *Hashtags*, such as *#climatechange*, for example, make it simple for other people to find all the tweets on a particular subject. The hashtag is included within a tweet.

Sending a Tweet

Tap the **New Tweet** icon on the Twitter Home Screen and shown on the right. Then start typing your message, replacing **What's happening?**, as shown on the next page.

The following icons are shown above.

Use the camera to take a photo to insert in the tweet.

Broadcast live to your followers, after downloading the *Periscope* app.

Insert an existing picture from your Gallery.

Include a *GIF* (*Graphics Interchange Format*) i.e. *animated image* in the tweet.

Ask a question for other people to vote on in a *poll*.

Use the phone's *GPS system* to include your current *location* in the tweet.

When the tweet is finished, tap the Tweet button, as shown at the top of this page.

Responding to a Tweet

Your followers can respond to a tweet by tapping any of the following icons, along the bottom of the tweet.

WhatsApp

This is a free messaging service, designed for phones, and having over a billion users worldwide. Your WhatsApp contacts must be on your phone contacts list and have WhatsApp Messenger installed from their app store.

WhatsApp Messenger is a free app which can be installed from the Play Store. Downloading and installing apps is discussed in Chapter 10.

WhatsApp

Some of the main features of WhatsApp are:

- Free worldwide telephone calls using your Internet connection.
- Sending and receiving photos, videos, voice messages and documents files.
- Group chats with friends, family, colleagues, etc.
- Share your current *location* in a message.
- WhatsApp uses your phone number rather than a username, password or PIN, etc.

Using WhatsApp

Tap the WhatsApp icon on the Apps or Home screen, as shown at the top right above.

The three main sections are **CHATS**, **STATUS** and **CALLS**, as shown below.

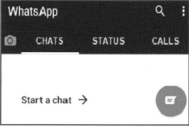

Tap the green icon shown on the right and on the previous page to select a contact and start a **CHAT**. You can either type or speak a text message, or select either a video call or voice only call.

Icons Used in WhatsApp CHATS

Video call   Voice only call

Add an emoji   Take a photo or video

Attach media, etc., as shown on the right

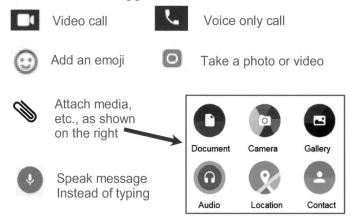

Document   Camera   Gallery

Audio   Location   Contact

Speak message Instead of typing

The **STATUS** option shown on page 164 is used to send text messages, photos and animated GIFs that disappear after 24 hours.

Select **CALLS** shown on page 164 and then tap the icon shown on the right to start a voice or video call with contacts who have WhatsApp installed.

Instagram

This is a very popular social network owned by Facebook and installed free from the Play Store. Among its many features are:

- You build a *Profile*, containing messages, photos and videos taken with the *camera* feature.
- Other people can follow you and view your profile. Instagram suggests other people for you to follow.
- Instagram has powerful photo editing tools and filters.
- *Stories* are messages and photos which disappear from your profile after 24 hours.
- Search for person, place or subject to display a scrollable *Gallery* of multiple photos and videos.

Snapchat

Snapshot is another free app for sharing photos, videos and text between phones and is especially popular with young people. Some of its special features are:

- Messages are free and are sent to any of your phone contacts or anyone you add as friends.
- Tap to take photo, hold to make a video.
- Set the viewing time from 1 to 10 seconds.
- Send to your chosen recipients.
- Messages, photos and videos ("snaps") disappear up to 10 seconds after your contact has viewed them.
- You can edit and draw on photos and add captions.
- Snapchat *Stories* are photos and videos which can be viewed repeatedly up to 24 hours after posting them.
- Your Stories are visible in your Stories section and in your friends' Stories sections.

Managing Your Phone

Introduction

This chapter discusses various topics involving the use of the Internet and also the security of your phone and its data. These topics include:

- Using the *Clouds* on the Internet for the storage and backup of your photos and data files.

- Accessing your cloud storage from any phone or computer, from anywhere in the world where you can connect to the Internet.

- E-mailing a *link* to allow a contact to access files such as photos or documents from the clouds.

- Printing from your phone over the Internet to a remote printer.

- Using *mobile data* and *mobile hotspots*.

- Avoiding the dangers of *data roaming*.

- *Downloading*, *uploading* and *streaming* files.

- Security including Lock Screen options.

- Backing up important files, encryption, e-mail scams and changing your password regularly.

- Tracing a lost or stolen phone.

Cloud Computing

This has been a huge development in recent years. Copies of your photos and other files are stored on your phone and *synced* to storage in the clouds on the Internet. The latter consists of Internet server computers managed by large companies around the world. Well known cloud storage systems include Google Drive, Dropbox and OneDrive.

Some of the advantages of cloud storage are:

- The clouds act as very safe backup storage for your photos and other files, managed by computing professionals.

- You can access your files from any computer with an Internet connection, anywhere in the world.

- You can transfer files between different computers in different locations and between different types of computer — smartphone, tablet, laptop and desktop.

- Previously this was done by copying files and photos, etc., onto a floppy disc or more recently flash drives or memory sticks.

- You can easily share a copy of a file or photo with a friend or colleague by e-mail from your cloud folder or by sending a link in an e-mail.

As an example, in writing a book such as this one, I take screenshots of my Android phone which are automatically saved in the **Photos** folder on the phone. From here they can be *shared* to OneDrive, Google Drive or Dropbox for inclusion in the text of the book in Microsoft Publisher on my PC desktop computer.

Share

In a similar way I use OneDrive to transfer files between my desktop computer, laptop computer and phone, which I use in different locations. Once you've saved and *closed* a document or photo on one machine it is automatically synced to your cloud storage, e.g. OneDrive and then downloaded to the *local storage* on all your other devices on which OneDrive is installed. This is very useful now that Microsoft's world leading programs such as Word and Excel are available on Android phones.

OneDrive, DropBox and Google Drive can be freely installed on an Android phone from the PlayStore.

On other computers:

- Install Google Drive from **www.drive.google.com**
- Install Dropbox from **www.dropbox.com**
- OneDrive is pre-installed on Windows 10 machines.

You are initially allowed a limited amount of free storage space as shown below:

Dropbox: 2GB   OneDrive: 10GB   Google Drive: 15GB

Heavy users and businesses can pay to obtain extra storage.

How Safe are the Clouds?

Depending on your settings, deleting a file or photo from your phone may also remove the copy in the clouds. Also, some businesses feel wary of entrusting important files to other companies around the world. So to be extra sure of keeping crucial data and irreplaceable photos secure, it's advisable to make additional backups on removable media such as CDs, DVDs and flash drives or memory sticks.

Backing Up Photos to the Clouds

When you take a photo using the **Camera** app on your phone, it is automatically saved on the Internal Storage of your phone and can be viewed immediately using the **Photos** app. A copy of the photo should also be quickly backed up or *synced* automatically to the **My Drive** folder in Google Drive in the clouds. So your photos should be viewable on any computer on the Internet, signed in to your Google Account, as discussed on page 42 onwards.

To make sure your photos are backed up to Google Drive, tap the **Photos** icon and tap **Settings** from the menu button.

Photos   ☰ Menu   ⚙ Settings

Backup & sync should be switched **On** as shown on the left below and then your Google account should be displayed.

Back up & sync ⬤	Backup & sync
	Backing up to jillbrown@gmail.com

Downloading, Uploading and Streaming

These terms refer to *files* such as photos, documents, music and videos.

- When a file is *downloaded* it is *copied* from the clouds and *saved* on your phone's Internal Storage.

- *Uploading* copies files from a phone and *saves* them in the clouds, for backup or sharing purposes.

- When music or a video is *streamed* it is transferred from the clouds in a *continuous flow* for you to listen to or watch immediately. A streamed file is *not saved* on your phone's Internal Storage.

- *Syncing* refers to the *automatic* downloading and uploading of files.

Google Cloud Printing

Google Cloud Print is an app which allows any computer, such as an Android smartphone, to print photos or documents over the Internet to a printer also connected to the Internet. Cloud Print is a free app in the Google Play Store and can be installed as discussed in Chapter 10.

To set up a printer connected to a laptop or desktop PC, so that you can print to it from anywhere using your phone:

On the PC:

- Open **Google Chrome** on the PC.
- Tap **Settings**, **Advanced**, **Google Cloud Print**.
- Tap **Add printers** and select the printer.

To print from your phone:

- In the main **Settings**, under **Printing**, make sure **Cloud Print** is **On**.

- Open the photo, e-mail, or document, etc., then tap the 3-dot menu and select **Print**.

- Select your printer from the drop-down menu and then tap the print icon shown on the right and below.

EPSON XP-312 3...

Copies: 1   Paper size: A4 210 x 297...

HP ePrint

This is a cloud printing service developed by Hewlett-Packard, for use with smartphones, tablet computers and laptops, etc. A free *HP ePrint* app is available in the Play Store. The system requires an HP ePrint compatible Wi-Fi printer registered to the HP ePrint cloud service called *HP ePrint Center*. This assigns a unique e-mail address to the printer.

The document to be printed is attached to an e-mail sent to the e-mail address of the ePrinter.

Using ePrinters in Public Locations

HP ePrint can also be used by people on the move who need to print while away from the home or office. This uses a number of *HP ePrint Public Print* locations in, for example, hotels and airports, etc. These allow the users of a smartphone or tablet to print documents (for a fee) while travelling. HP ePrint uses GPS to list hotels, etc., providing public printing facilities in a particular area.

Sending a Link to a File or Photo

You can send a *link* to a file or photo stored in the clouds in an e-mail so that a friend can easily open and view it.

- Open the file in the cloud storage system such as OneDrive or Google Drive.
- Tap **Share** or **Share & export**. **Share**
- Tap **Copy link**.
- Open the Gmail app and enter the e-mail text, etc.
- Tap and hold then **Paste** the link into the e-mail.
- **Send** the e-mail.
- The recipient can then tap the link to open the file and view the photo, email, or document, etc.

Mobile Data

Mobile Data allows you to connect a smartphone to the Internet using the phone's 3G/4G cell phone network, in places where you can't access Wi-Fi.

Mobile data can be switched on after selecting **Settings** and **Data usage**, as shown below.

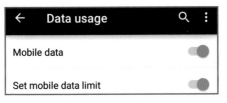

Once **Mobile data** is **On** you can use the Internet to transfer data such as e-mails, Web pages, photos, music etc.

However, mobile data is more expensive than Wi-Fi, which should be used whenever possible. As shown above, it's possible to set a limit to the amount of mobile data you can use. This could prevent you receiving very large, unexpected bills. (Not a problem if you have a *data plan* allowing *unlimited data*.)

Data Roaming

When travelling abroad and out of range of your own phone network, *data roaming* connects your phone to an overseas network for using the Internet with mobile data. Some travellers inadvertently ran up bills of thousands of pounds, until 2017 European regulations set a limit of £50 a month. Outside of the EU it may still be possible to run up a large bill. To avoid this risk, when travelling abroad:

- Tap **Settings> More> Mobile Networks**.
- Make sure **Data roaming** is **Off**.
- Use the free Wi-Fi in hotels and cafes, etc.

Setting Up a Mobile Hotspot

With **Mobile data On**, as discussed on page 173, your phone can be used to connect a tablet, laptop or desktop computer to the Internet in places where there is no Wi-Fi.

- From the **Settings** menu on your phone, under **Wireless & networks**, select **More** then **Tethering & mobile hotspot**.

- Switch on **Mobile Wi-Fi hotspot**, tap **Set up Wi-Fi hotspot** shown below.

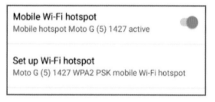

- Enter a **Password** for the hotspot, as shown below on the left, and tap **SAVE**.

- Tap the Wi-Fi icon on your tablet, laptop, etc.

- Select your phone from the list of available networks on a tablet, laptop, etc., as shown below right for my **Moto G (5)** phone.

- Select **Connect** on the tablet, laptop, or desktop, etc., to start using the Internet via your phone.

Please note: Using your phone as a mobile hotspot will increase your use of data and drain the battery quickly.

Security

The Android operating system has a number of security features as shown on the left below. These are displayed by tapping **Settings** followed by **Security**. .

Various options for the **Screen lock** can be used to prevent other people from using your phone when it first starts up.

- Tap **Screen lock** shown above, then choose from creating a **Pattern**, entering a **PIN** or a **Password**.

- **Fingerprint**, discussed on page 46, appears after you've set one of the other options such as **Pattern**, **PIN** or **Password**.

- **Smart Lock** shown above keeps your phone unlocked when it detects it is safe to do so, in a trusted place, on your body or using facial recognition, for example.

- **Encryption** shown above *scrambles* all the data on your phone. It can only be deciphered by someone knowing your **PIN** or **Password**, etc.

- Setting a **SIM card lock** means a **PIN** is needed to use the phone for calls or cellular data.

Further Security Precautions

- Choose obscure passwords and change them regularly.

- Do not give passwords, credit card or account details in reply to e-mails or telephone calls.

- If you forget your password you can usually reset it by tapping **Forgot password?** A *link to a Web site* will be e-mailed to you, allowing you to reset the password.

- Professionally managed *cloud storage systems* such as Google Drive, Dropbox and Microsoft OneDrive, provide useful backup copies of your files.

- Also make backup copies of important files on *removable media* such as *flash drives* or on CDs or DVDs. Such files might include legal or financial documents or irreplaceable photos of major events.

Finding a Lost or Stolen Phone

- Open the **Google** search program on any computer you are signed into with your Google account.

- Enter **Find my phone** in the Google Search Bar on the computer and press **Enter**.

- Enter the password for your Google account and select **NEXT**.

- Google displays the location of your phone on a map and gives you options to **PLAY SOUND** on your phone for 5 minutes, **LOCK** the phone or **ERASE** all content or data from your phone.

- There are also several apps in the Google Play Store to track a lost or stolen phone.

Index